"Brave, practical, and true, Liz shares her magical journey for anyone brave enough (and generous enough) to want to go on the journey of a lifetime."

Seth Godin

"I met Liz more than a decade ago in Gulu, Uganda. *Beginner's Pluck* is a thoughtful book about what Liz has been strategically doing in the world, not merely optimistically hoping for. Her authentic voice is one I trust because I've seen what she's done. As you flip these pages, you won't want to be more like Liz. Instead, you'll want to figure out what your next steps are to release your passions, hopes, and love into a world which is in desperate need of someone just like you to engage it."

Bob Goff, hon. consul for the Republic of Uganda and author
New York Times bestsellers *Love Does* and *Everybody Always*

"I am SO VERY GLAD this book exists. We have long needed Liz's expert voice speaking into the minds of dreamers and doers, the ones who have the ideas and want to execute, and the ones who are exhaustedly executing. We want purpose in our day, and Liz does it with her life and teaches it here."

Annie F. Downs, bestselling author of *100 Days to Brave*
and *Remember God*

"Witty and full of brilliant insight, Liz Bohannon delivers a much-needed antidote to a Western mindset careening between youthful entitlement and shame/fear-based inertia. Most of us who dream to be extraordinary have never learned first to be ordinary."

Wm Paul Young, author of *The Shack, Cross Road, Eve,*
and *Lies We Believe about God*

"Liz's words, full of wit and inspiration, felt as though my best girlfriend pulled me in close for a lesson in life. As if she were writing just to me and declaring, 'You are enough.' Liz's honesty and candor about her journey of creating something bigger than herself are inspiring, practical, and life-giving."

Jamie Ivey, host of *The Happy Hour with Jamie Ivey* podcast
and author of the bestselling book *If You Only Knew: My
Unlikely Unavoidable Story of Becoming Free*

"*Beginner's Pluck* is a guide to living *with purpose*, believing we were created *on purpose*. Far from the exhausting message of 'hustle harder,' Liz invites us into the winsome adventure of building a life of passion, impact, and living into who we are created to be."

Rebekah Lyons, author of *You Are Free*

"*Beginner's Pluck* is the life map I wish I could have read decades ago. Liz is a shining example of the imperfect purpose we all aspire to do and be. WOW, what an authentic example to us all."

Jeff Shinabarger, founder of Plywood People

"*Beginner's Pluck* is a breath of fresh air for dream chasers and passion people everywhere. Liz has a way of expressing and articulating that make you feel as though you are sitting across from her, enthralled by her raw and tangible insight and life experience. These words are necessary food for the soul for anyone feeling stuck, inadequate, or buried under the necessary pressure to be perfect. Brava, brava."

Arielle Estoria, poet, speaker, and author

"Free-spirited, honest, humble, willing to ask the difficult questions, and insightful, Liz leads by showing her humanity. Looking for a life of purpose and passion? *Beginner's Pluck* gives tangible directions you can incorporate in your life right now. Liz is a disruptive storyteller whose words just might help you do the work to return home to yourself."

Chidimma Ozor, podcaster, educator, disruptive storyteller, and founder of conscious + aligned

"The transformative force that Liz Forkin Bohannon is fiercely shines on every page of this book. *Beginner's Pluck* is the catalytic push and heart check we need to boldly choose purpose over popularity and to live our lives not to impress but to make impact—REAL, lasting impact. Liz shares invaluable insights that cleverly disrupt norms so prevalent throughout culture today, exposing stale perceptions of success while freeing us to thrive in purposeful lives built with intention, gut-honest truth, and creativity. Liz's story will no doubt fuel an unleashing of world changers disbanding fear, owning average, and accomplishing the extraordinary."

Kanita Benson, founder of She Saves a Nation

Beginner's Pluck

Beginner's Pluck

BUILD YOUR LIFE OF PURPOSE AND IMPACT NOW

LIZ FORKIN BOHANNON

BakerBooks

a division of Baker Publishing Group
Grand Rapids, Michigan

Published by Baker Books
a division of Baker Publishing Group
PO Box 6287, Grand Rapids, MI 49516-6287
www.bakerbooks.com

Printed in the United States of America

Library of Congress Cataloging-in-Publication Control Number: 2019006889

978-0-8010-9424-8 (cloth)
978-1-5409-0022-7 (ITPE)

19 20 21 22 23 24 25   7 6 5 4 3 2 1

For my incredibly loving and supportive parents,
who never clipped my wings.

For my boys,
who are my home and my greatest adventure.

For the Dreamer/Doers
(and especially those who flail
and stumble a bit along the way):
you are my inspiration.

Contents

Contents

Introduction

Naked and Afraid

was taking a shower—the public kind that you have to keep feeding quarters—in a national park in Northern California at about 6 AM. If you didn't know that pay-by-the-minute showers existed, you're welcome for this educational book about the gritty wonders of the world I'm writing for you. Stick with me, kid.

I was in my midtwenties and I'd been on the road with my brand-new husband living out of our Honda Element for about four months. We had a meeting with a potential buyer (Of what? We'll get to that later; details, details.) in a few hours that I was trying to get spiffed up for. And by "spiffed up" I mean, I washed my hair for the first time in a week and cleaned the peanut butter crust out from under my fingernails.

I was thankful for an actual, real shower with running water (versus a slightly moistened towelette bath in a McDonald's bathroom—my norm at the time), and I was going to town sudsing up my hair, singing Carole King's "Natural

Woman," when . . . the water turns off, really messing with my *American Idol* shower vibes. But not to worry! It just needs another quarter.

Only,

I'm fresh out of quarters this time.

Of course.

So here I am. Naked and afraid. OK. Not so much "afraid" as angry. It's cold and I'm covered in soap and I have no water and I need to be at this meeting in San Francisco in two hours and it's at least an hour and a half away.

I have no plan.

So, I cuss a bunch and then I start to cry. (Alternate title of this book.) Not so much about the meeting or even because of the soap in my eyes, but because all of a sudden I go from singing Carole King and being grateful for an actual real shower to looking at this frozen-in-time snapshot of my life trajectory.

Yes, I was stranded in the shower with soap in my eyes. But it wasn't just that. I also had no income, no insurance, and no home address. I had spent the entire day before The Shower Incident as a vendor at a hipster street market where I made a whopping $11, which was barely enough to cover the cost of the jar of peanut butter I consumed throughout the grueling 12-hour day of near-constant rejection, let alone the cost of my market booth and the gas it took to get there. Being stranded in the shower was really just icing on the pathetic cake. This is not what I pictured when my parents and teachers and coaches told me I "could be whatever [I] wanted to be."

Perhaps you've also had a sense that you are not where you'd hoped you'd be by now: the dream job, the forever partner, the financial security, the supportive community, a sense of purpose and meaning in your days. Perhaps you have a sneaking suspicion that you were made for more and you're not quite sure when you managed to wander off the straight and narrow path toward The Promised Land of Your Purpose and Passion.

Here's the brutal truth no one wants to tell you: "Following Your Dreams" and "Finding Your Passion" and "Dreaming Big" sometimes land you broke, naked, and crying by yourself in a bathroom made of cinderblocks in the middle of the woods.

THE END.

Just kidding, friends! That's not the end. (And in fact, it's not really the beginning, either. We'll make our way back there at some point.)

But right now, I want to tell you that if you are reading this while metaphorically naked and stranded, you're not alone. It might actually be a sign that you're on to something really good. (But if you are *literally* naked and stranded, I bless your decision to burn this book to fuel your rescue smoke-signal efforts.)

In fact, that feeling of being lost, empty-handed, and clueless that you've been taught to panic over or fake your way through might actually be a hint that you're in *a really good place*.

What if feeling lost or stuck because of your lack of experience, confidence, connections, and know-how was not a hindrance but instead a secret weapon in your journey to building a life of purpose and impact?

What if, without even knowing it, you've got a special power that you just need to acknowledge and then learn how to wield to your advantage?

That magic power, my friends?

Beginner's Pluck.

According to some official-enough looking website on the internet, **Beginner's LUCK** is defined as "*the phenomenon of novices experiencing disproportionate frequency of success or succeeding against an expert in a given activity. One would expect experts to outperform novices—when the opposite happens it is counter-intuitive, hence the need for a term to describe this phenomenon.*"[1]

Phenomenon. That's the word we're using to describe when a Beginner actually succeeds. Ouch. Kinda harsh. Yet, when I look at my own story and the hundreds of stories I've heard over the last ten years while meeting people doing meaningful work and creating a positive impact, the Beginner's success story doesn't actually seem to be all that rare. Certainly not a phenomenon.

In fact, the story of the empty-handed, know-nothing, pie-in-the-sky Beginner actually creating an extraordinary life of passion and purpose is common enough to make me wonder: Do Beginners succeed despite their lack of experience? Or perhaps, in part, because of it? Could being a Beginner (or at least, acting like one by channeling your Inner Beginner during every season of life) actually be an asset in your journey to build a life of purpose and passion?

Yes!

After all, who needs luck when you've got PLUCK?* What many beginners lack in experience, track record, know-how,

*If you're not a 90-year-old woman named Dottie who learned to speak English in 1908, you may not know that *pluck* is one of the best words in the English language.

and connections, they make up in nerve, curiosity, spirit, courage, and a willingness to acknowledge they don't have it all figured out. Which are all, as it turns out, incredibly useful in building lives of purpose, passion, and impact.

If you're feeling lost, overwhelmed, and clueless, it can feel like a pretty demoralizing place to be.

But.

It's actually a miraculous place to be.

You, my friend, should you choose to accept this ~~mission~~ mentality, are in the Magical Land of Beginners. It's the alternate universe where falling doesn't hurt as much because you don't have that far to tumble.

It's a world where all the energy you would have spent posturing and being afraid and desperately trying to save face and keep up with the Joneses can be poured into building a meaningful life that aligns with your truest beliefs and deepest desires.

If you learn a few key principles of truly owning your Beginner's Pluck and are *intentional* about cultivating those mindsets along the journey, your chances of success in building this kind of life might actually be better than the fancy, experienced, well-connected Know-It-Alls.

In the years between being stranded in the shower in the woods questioning all my life choices and my present-day reality of living into my purpose, I've learned a thing or two about not finding but *building* a life of purpose, passion, and impact.

Yes, when used as a verb, it is what you do to that unsightly and embarrassing chin hair your partner still doesn't know about because you pluck (v.) in privacy, but the real magic is in the noun usage. Pluck (n.) means: spirited and determined courage. Synonyms: courage, bravery, nerve, backbone, spine, daring, spirit, intrepidity, fearlessness, mettle, grit, determination, fortitude, resolve, stout-heartedness, dauntlessness, valor, heroism, audacity.

❊ ❊ ❊

Hi. My name is Liz. I'm a wife and a mom and a journalist-gone-entrepreneur. I am the co-founder and CEO of a global socially-conscious fashion brand called Sseko (Say-Ko)* Designs that is creating community and opportunity for thousands of women in Uganda, the U.S., and across the globe. In addition to running a global company with employees and partners that span five continents, I've majorly pitted out on the dance floor while cutting a rug with *the* Ben and Jerry. During the first ever U.S.–Africa Leader's Summit, I listened, with tears rushing down my face, as First Ladies Laura Bush and Michelle Obama recognized Agnes, our brilliant managing director in Uganda, as a picture of "The Modern African Woman."

I've stood on stage at the Rockefeller Center, nine months pregnant, smiling through contractions while I received a surprise, giant cardboard check that I then carried with me as I waddled down 5th Ave and tried to hail a cab. I've gotten a little sassy on national television in front of 7 million people and stood in an airport magazine shop flipping through *Vogue* magazine to see our stunning products featured on a glossy spread.

I've started out the day negotiating a trade deal in a smoky back room filled with men who didn't believe that as a woman I should have a place at the (literal) table and somehow ended up closing the deal at the United Arab Emirates' equivalent of Disney World at 1 AM, eating caramel corn and riding roller coasters with those same guys.

*The brand name Sseko is derived from the Luganda word "Enseko," which means laughter.

Over the last ten years, we've built one of the largest manufacturing companies in Uganda, where we've entertained the president on multiple occasions, proving to him in person the magic (and gross domestic product!) women can create when actually taken seriously and given the opportunity to thrive in industries traditionally dominated by men.

And yet, I can promise you that none of these epic and rewarding highlights compare to the simple, everyday, even mundane moments that are fueled with belief that the work I am doing matters. That—with plenty of failures and missteps along the way—I am actively co-creating the world I want to live in.

As part of my work, I've had the privilege of traveling the globe from rural Kentucky to Estonia,* speaking to and hearing from tens of thousands of people about their desires to live lives of purpose and impact. I've interviewed hundreds of people looking for meaningful vocational opportunity, and through these experiences, I've been learning firsthand how the ubiquitous "Follow Your Dreams" and "Find Your Passion" motivational narrative is *really* affecting people.

And I've got to tell you: I think we've got some things very wrong. What I think was meant to be a message of encouragement and empowerment is actually creating anxiety, fear, and serious analysis paralysis.

My goal with this book is to teach you the principles that will help you debunk these myths, not so that you can live a

---

*I for sure had to look Estonia up on the map when I got invited to speak there, so if you're feeling bad about your European geography skills, join the club. Subsequently, a few weeks later I was invited to come speak in Georgia and automatically assumed I was blowing up in the European market. No offense to my fellow Americans, but I was sorely disappointed (and embarrassed) when, after inquiring about whether I'd need a visa to get into Georgia, I realized they were referring to the state, not the country.

life of complacency but so that you can stop wasting your time hunting for a unicorn that doesn't exist and instead get down to the incredibly juicy, adventurous, life-giving work of *building* an extraordinary life of passion, purpose, and impact.

Over the last ten years, I've taken notes and boiled down hundreds of conversations and stories and interviews to 14 key principles that guide my life and allow me to access the counterintuitive magic of Beginner's Pluck. Building a life of purpose and impact is not nearly as angsty and unachievable and overwhelming as you think it is. It's not rocket science. (But there is science!) In fact, it's probably simpler than you can imagine. It's Beginner's work, after all.

The principles of Beginner's Pluck:

1. Own Your Average
2. Stop Trying to "Find Your Passion"
3. Dream Small
4. Choose Curiosity over Criticism
5. Be on Assignment in Your Own Life
6. Find and Replace
7. Surprise Yourself
8. Get Your Steps In
9. Get Hooked on Making (and Keeping!) Promises
10. Be Good with Good Enough
11. Stop, Drop, and WOW
12. Dream to Attract Your Team
13. Don't Hide from The Shadows
14. Walk One Another Home

Listen, I believe in the very core of my being that you were made to be here, right now, right where you are. There is something extraordinarily wonderful and mindbogglingly awesome about you. Not about what you've done, or are doing, or will do, but just about who you are and who you were created to be. Like a strand of DNA, you are a unique sequence of The Divine, and therefore you will leave an imprint on the world in a way that no one else on Planet Earth can. And every day that you spend being paralyzed by fear is one less day that we get to experience the gifts you have to give.

Our vocations are an incredibly important part of building a life of purpose and impact because, as Annie Dillard says, "Where we spend our days is, of course, how we spend our lives."[2] I will explore the principles of Beginner's Pluck by using my story and specifically my experience building a social enterprise from the ground up over the last ten years. But let me be very clear: you needn't be an entrepreneur to benefit from the principles of Beginner's Pluck.

These 14 principles apply to all vocations; and our vocations are not just where and how we get paid, but every area of life where we are pursuing our purpose and creating an impact. In order to access your Beginner's Pluck, these principles can and should be applied not only in your jobs but in your creative endeavors, family, community, and inner lives.

You can use the principles of Beginner's Pluck to build a life of purpose and impact while raising nonprofit funds *and* while raising teenagers.

You can do it while closing deals *and* while closing the educational gap.

You can do it while building companies *and* while building LEGO towers.

You can do it while running for office *and* while running your first 5K.

You can do it while nursing patients in a hospital *and* while nursing a wee babe, bleary-eyed at 3 AM.

You can do it while speaking from a stage to thousands of people *and* while you bravely speak your truth out loud in the mirror to yourself.

BUT . . .

You cannot do it if you're living in fear.

You cannot do it if you're running someone else's race.

You cannot do it accidentally.

If you want to build a life of purpose, it's going to have to be *on purpose*.

❋ ❋ ❋

For all of you who are done playing small, done being ruled by your insecurities, done wasting precious time and energy wondering where you belong and comparing and scrolling and tapping and wishing . . .

For the Misfit, the Space Cadet, the Wild One, the Misunderstood . . .

For the Scaredy Cat, the Never Enough, the Can't Keep Up . . .

For the Too Much, Too Messy, Too Big, Too Tender . . .

For the one who is ready to put a sleeper hold on all of the above and get down to the BIG BUSINESS of creating, unleashing, and saying YES to adventure . . .

IT'S TIME TO OWN YOUR INNER BEGINNER.

I'll be here to cheer you on.

You're not alone.

You can sit with us. Right next to me.

[Gently but enthusiastically pats seat on the lunch table bench that's borderline uncomfortably close.*]

Now, are you ready to get to work and have some fun?

---

*Don't worry, although we left off in my journey with me naked, sudsy, and stranded in the woods, by this point in the story I am now fully clothed.

ONE

Own Your Average

When I was in elementary school, I tried out for the community theatre production of *Cinderella* and auditioned for the role of—you guessed it—Cinderella. I mean, go big or go home, right?

And I landed it! And the show eventually made its way from rural Illinois to New York where I was the youngest lead to ever grace a Broadway stage.

Oh, Liz Forkin Bohannon! The musical theatre child prodigy! I think I saw a special on Bravo about her once, you perhaps thought to yourself while browsing the shelves of your local bookstore.

Just kidding. You'd likely never heard my name before because here is how that audition *actually* went down: I went up against seasoned high-school-aged thespians for the role of Cinderella. My mother, a very intelligent woman who surely recognized the unlikelihood of a "successful" outcome, did not try to persuade me otherwise. In fact, she practiced my song with me, drove me to the audition, and whispered a hopeful and sincere "Break a leg, Lizzy Pea!" as I walked through the curtains into the spotlight on an empty stage in front of four scary-looking judges. I gave it my best go and afterward my mom took me to McDonald's for a celebratory ice cream cone.

In the few days between the audition and receiving a call from the casting director, I threw my eight-year-old self into a Cinderella character study. I dreamed about the costume changes and the lights and determined where I could surreptitiously pinch myself to illicit enough pain to squeeze out some fake, award-winning tears. A few days into my preparation for my dream role, we got a phone call from the director. I indeed had made the cast!

My role was . . .

Bird.

I did not, in fact, have a single line in the entire play. Just a few scenes where I'd hop around on stage with a handful of other mediocre wannabe woodland animals.

A BIRD.

A bird who didn't even have a NAME.

I was *devastated*.

When my mom relayed the news, I burst into tears and ran into her bedroom closet, shutting myself in and sobbing in the dark. I was, of course, sad about my dashed dreams, but I also remember the feeling of being utterly *humiliated*.

I replayed in my head all the practice that went into that audition. All the unabashed dreaming out loud about what it would be like to be Cinderella. I couldn't believe I was so *stupid* to want something that bad and to actually believe I had a chance.

After a few minutes of sobbing by myself, my mom opened the closet door and sat down with me while I cried. She scratched my back and told me that she was proud of me for trying. And then, through my tears, I verbalized what was surely assumed by all parties: I would not be participating in that stupid play, *obviously*.

And then my sweet, supportive, back-scratching mama sat up straight and made it *very clear* that actually that was *not* how this was going to go down.* I had auditioned, and I had received a role. And I was *not allowed* to quit because it wasn't the starring role I had imagined. She told me that practices started on Monday and that I would *absolutely be* attending. Case closed.

And then she told me that sure, it stung to be a bird when you wanted to be Cinderella, but that I would be the best non-speaking bird that stage had ever seen.

She echoed the famous show-biz words of Constantin Stanislavski. "There are no small parts," she said. "Only small actors."[1]

She promised me that she'd help make me an epic bird costume, and sitting there in that dark closet, we brainstormed a character name because while I couldn't change my role, I could at least have some fancy feathers and the dignity of having a character name that wasn't just a species classification.

We went back and forth for a while and finally decided on "Biddy Bird." It was no matter that this "character name" would never reach beyond the two of us or even make it into the official program.

When the time came for opening night, I Biddy Bird-ed my heart out. I sang loudly, hopped endlessly, and even managed

---

*My mom is #MomGoals. Reminder to all parents, myself included, to let your kids dream big and don't bail them out when they fail.

to depart from the official choreography for a second and shake my fancy tail feathers like the rebel, avant-garde, avian-inspired thespian that I was.

I would love to tell you that this role prepared me for my next slightly better role and so on and so forth until I managed to build a successful theatre career. But in fact, the very next play I tried out for was *Babes in Toyland* where I landed the role of . . .

AND I KID YOU NOT

A moth.

I mean, if there is anything more demoralizing than a nameless bird, it's most certainly "moth." The path to being demoted from a non-speaking bird is a narrow one, but I managed to find and walk it.

I mean, A MOTH?!

But I digress.

The point of that experience was not, in fact, to prepare me for a slightly better role and launch me into the eventual Broadway success I dreamed about. Rather, it taught me that we are neither called to vie for the spotlight nor to shrink into the chorus line. We are simply called to figure out what we have to offer,

the gift *we* have to give,
the words *we* have to speak,
the art *we* have to make,
the song *we* have to sing,

and then go *all in* and belt it out like a buck-toothed eight-year-old trying to win a Tony award for a non-speaking role in a community theatre production.

26

* * *

We each have a sacred part to play. What the world *doesn't* need are more people who are desperately trying to convince themselves and others they are *above average* special Cinderellas because they think that is what will earn them the spotlight and that the spotlight itself will give them a sense of worthiness and purpose.

The world *also* doesn't need more people who shrink into the chorus line because they erroneously believe they are inherently *below average* and are terrified of what others might think of them should they spread their wings and try to fly.

Because the truth is, you're, like me, most likely . . .

Pretty average.

I know, I know. I have a real gift for inspiring words. Please someone make a beautiful hand-lettered Insta-Quote out of that:

You. Are. Average.

The Almighty Bell Curve

-woohoo!

But it's true. The majority of people reading (and writing) this book are most likely somewhere in the middle of the Almighty Bell Curve when it comes to inherent talent, capacity, giftedness, and intelligence.

If that makes you feel bad, it's because we've been conditioned to think that being inherently average is depressing and demoralizing. When in fact, Owning Your Average is actually a *remarkably freeing and powerful* acknowledgment because being born inherently gifted or above average isn't a prerequisite to living an extraordinary life.

Let me be very clear: Owning Your Average is *not* a call for complacency. Don't you dare Own Your Average so that you can stay there or so that you can be content with an average life devoid of passion, purpose, connection, or deep meaning. Own Your Average so that you can *free yourself up* from the junk sucking up all the energy you spend trying to figure out how you measure up and instead channel that energy into becoming an interested, curious, Dreamer/Doer who believes that truly extraordinary stories and lives can be built by the Average Us.

Your inherent gifts and talents and smarts most likely do not make you above average. And neither do your fears and deepest insecurities and shortcomings. I hate to break it to you, but those are also, well, *quite average*. You do know that almost every. last. one of us deals with imposter syndrome, don't you? Am I good enough? Do I have what it takes? Will I be found out? What if I fail? What will other people think of me? Am I in over my head? I've literally never met a non-sociopathic human who doesn't struggle with self-doubt.

If you think your fears and limiting mindsets make you special, you're going to have to try harder than that, old sport!

Something miraculous will happen when you Own Your Average. You will stop only saying yes to the things you think you'll immediately excel in. When you Own Your Average, you start to realize that no one is thinking about you quite as much as you think they are. You are not Beyoncé. (Or maybe you are, in which case, OMG. HI, BEY!) When you decide to Own Your Average, you will start to believe that success will require lots and lots of work and isn't just an inevitable result of being born awesome. You also realize that your insecurities and failures aren't the telltale sign that you're below average. You know that mistakes and wrong turns are simply a requisite on the road to building an above-average life of purpose and passion, which means you'll be less afraid to fail and flail a bit.

And more importantly, you'll become less afraid and more likely to succeed, perhaps *wildly*, because you truly believe you're just as worthy and likely to build an extraordinary life of purpose and passion as anyone else.

* * *

I know it's only chapter one and it's a lot to ask that you trust me when I'm asking you to go against every self-helpy inspirational thing you've ever heard about how *special* you are and instead shout your Average from the rooftops. So, if you don't trust me quite enough yet, allow me to introduce The Scientists who will back me up.

There was a brilliant study done by a psychologist named Claudia M. Mueller that fundamentally changed the stories I tell myself, the way I run my company, and the way I raise my children. Way to go, CLAUDIA!

Claudia and her scientist pals gave a test to several hundred fifth graders.[2] After the first set of problems, on which most children did pretty well, they praised the children.

In Group One, they praised the kids for being really smart. "Wow! That's a great score! You must be *really smart and gifted. You're so special.*"

In Group Two, they praised progress, growth, and work ethic. "Wow! That's a great score! You must have *worked really hard* at solving those problems and stuck with it when someone else would have gotten frustrated and given up. I bet you'll do even better next time!"

The result? Those in Group One who were praised for their *inherent* talent and intelligence shied away from choosing a more challenging assignment in the future. Once the belief that they were special got planted, the risk of accepting a challenging assignment where they may struggle and fail became too great.

On the other hand, the students in Group Two who were praised for their progress, hard work, curiosity, grit, determination, and mindset wanted a *more* challenging assignment in the future. They were eager for the next challenge where they could continue to work hard and learn from the process. Failure wasn't nearly as scary to these kids.

Not only did the kids in Group One want easier assignments, their performance on the next test *declined*, while the kids from Group Two performed *markedly better.*

What I desperately want you to understand is that being extraordinary or talented or gifted isn't a prerequisite to living an extraordinary life and being a part of a story that is so much bigger than you. Building a life of purpose and passion has so much less to do with your inherent intelligence or gifts and more about your posture, mindset, and curiosity quotient. And not a single one of these things is limited to The Above Average among us. So, go against all the instinctive motivational mumbo jumbo you've ever heard and proudly . . .

Own Your Average!

❊ ❊ ❊

All this talk about Owning Your Average might have your insecurities flaring up a bit. I'm going to ask you to trust me again as we embark on a little experiment: every time you say or think you're struggling with an "insecurity" I want you to replace the word "insecurity" with "Immature Ego."

What? Ego? Me?! *The nerve of this lady* . . .

If talking about your Ego makes you feel defensive, allow me to redirect your aghast over to Franciscan friar and spiritual teacher Richard Rohr. Blame him!

Rohr says our Immature Egos are "a social and mental construct to get you started on your life journey. It is largely defined in distinction from others, precisely as your separate and unique self. It is probably necessary to get started, but it becomes problematic when you stop there and spend the rest of your life promoting and protecting it."

Our Immature Egos are also, problematically, "inadequate to the big questions of love, death, suffering, God or infinity." He goes on to say, "When you are connected to The Whole, you no longer need to protect or defend The Part. You are now connected to something inexhaustible."[3]

Connected to The Whole. Gives me goosebumps every time.

When you're connected to The Whole, you will realize that the story you are partaking in and coauthoring is SO VERY

BIG that you can no longer believe in a story *so small* that it has you in the very center. You will become more enamored with the Bigness of the Beautiful Story and what we can accomplish *together* than with your own individual performance in it.

On this journey to building a life of purpose and impact, I can all but promise that you will say and do the wrong thing. You will flail and you will fumble. And at times it will be such a train wreck, you will think you'll never recover from it. You'll probably beat yourself up and say terrible things to yourself that you wouldn't dare say to another human. But time and time again, you will wake up the next day to a sun that did not fall out of the sky in response to your mistake. This will happen over and over until you finally start to let go of your Immature Ego that whispers the lie that you're powerful enough to screw it all up for good.

Richard Rohr goes on to tell us that our Immature Egos are "more bogus than bad."[4]

I love this so much. What this tells me is that I can stop beating myself up about my Immature Ego and instead simply get on with the work of helping my Ego grow up a little bit so I can be a part of a bigger, juicier story. As you attempt to mature your Ego, please be kind and gentle with yourself the way you *gently* and *kindly* and *patiently* help a child grow and learn instead of attempting to fault and shame them into maturity. The process of maturing our Egos is lifelong work, so you don't need to be a jerk about it. Your Immature Ego *used* to suit you and serve a purpose. It's not evil or bad, it's just that as you grow into becoming part of The Whole, the Old Costume you constructed no longer fits.

When we stop being obsessed with the Almighty Bell Curve, always asking "How do I measure up?" we can instead put our energy into becoming who we were created to be and encouraging others toward the belief that *they* are also an irreplaceable part of The Whole. When you Own Your Average, you'll start to understand that *every* human on Planet Earth is a unique combination and sequence of The Divine and carries an equally valuable, one of a kind, never-going-to-see-it-again brand of magic.

We are each unique.

But we are not unique for being unique. (Mind bender, I know.)

When you start believing this about yourself, you will start to channel all the energy you recover from worrying about how you compare into a beautiful vision of collective ambition—dreams that will raise the tide, not just for yourself but for others too.

When you Own Your Average and do the intentional work of helping your Ego mature, you will take on greater challenges and say yes before you're ready because you're less terrified of failing and more interested in growth and *movement forward*. You get to channel every ounce of that *recovered* energy you used to spend protecting yourself and worrying about what other people will think into solving interesting problems and building an extraordinary life of purpose and impact for yourself and others. When you Own Your Average, you can take risks and finally take flight.

And you, Biddy Bird, in all your Average glory, were meant *to fly*.

TWO

Stop Trying to "Find Your Passion"

After my illustrious childhood theatre career peaked with my riveting performance as A MOTH, I started exploring my other options and took up gymnastics. I have a distinct memory of sitting in my friend Lauren's bedroom in the fifth grade, admiring her gleaming shelves of gymnastic trophies, plaques, ribbons, and medals. I'd get a burning feeling of jealousy while staring at her accolades and hearing her humble brag about her pre-dawn practices. I dreamt about what it would feel like to love something *that much.*

While I was working on perfecting my back walkover in Level 3 gymnastics at the local YMCA (completely average, one might say), Lauren was practicing her back tuck with a private coach at a fancy gym across town. By the fifth grade, she was a Level 8 gymnast, and word on the street was that Level 8 was "Pre-Olympic."*

---

*I mean technically, not to split semantic hairs, *it's not like I'm still stewing over this*, BUT unless you *are* Olympic we're all technically PRE-Olympic, aren't we?

I, on the other hand, at my first competitive gymnastics meet, completely blanked while running my little heart down the vault mat and did the wrong trick altogether during my maiden vault competition. I did a "squat-through" instead of the requisite front handspring.*

You know what doing a squat-through when you should have done a front handspring earns you in a gymnastics meet, no matter how dang good that squat-through may have been executed?

It earns you, an awkward ten-year-old in sparkly spandex and braces (on only her two-front teeth! This should be considered cruel and usual pre-teen punishment), the opportunity to stand in front of a crowd of strangers and friends, while, *one by one*, the judges hold up BIG FAT ZEROS on their scorecards.

That's what it gets you.

I remember staring at all those zeros while I tried to smile and hold back tears, as I mentally compared my line of zeroes to Lauren's gleaming shelves of trophies and wondered if I would ever find *my thing*.

Throughout the next ten years I found myself on a similarly unremarkable trajectory: I liked school and was smart, but nowhere close to valedictorian.† I could carry a tune but didn't love choir enough to put in the effort to learn how to read music and eventually was not invited back. I tried out for the soccer team and did actually barely make it, only to fracture my elbow when I got really bored during a game and started

---

*If you want to be visually stunned and leave yourself in awe of the sheer capacity and gravity-defying athleticism of someone capable of doing a "squat-through," just Google it. You can thank me later for the athletic inspiration.

†Not prove my point, but how old were you when you realized that it's valedictorian and not valid*victorian*? Because I was TODAY YEARS OLD.

practicing my pirouette turns and took a cleat-induced fall, AS SERIOUS ATHLETES DO.

I was not on a promising track to find *my thing*. The thing that would light my little heart on fire.

As I left behind visions of literal trophies and awards and progressed toward adulthood, I started to think that because I was clearly not extraordinarily *passionate* at any one thing, this would certainly preclude me from living an extraordinary life.

I wonder if you've ever felt the same pang of insecurity and shame that comes from recognizing you might be semi-decent and enjoy a few things but that you haven't yet found *your thing*?

I seem to meet a lot of people plagued by this same insecurity and it's got me wondering: Where exactly it is that we get the idea that we need to have *our thing*? Did it emerge around the same time as this notion of a *soul mate*?

Perhaps without articulating it, do you secretly believe that your purpose and passion is a singular "soul mate" out there waiting for you to *discover* it? That there is *one* path that will lead you into its awe-inducing, fix-all-of-your-problems, forever embrace?

Looking back on my journey, I think I *did* believe that. And in retrospect, it's easy to see what an unproductive, anxiety-producing load of crap that is. To believe that your passion and purpose exists, fully formed "out there" like the handsome Italian moped–driving love interest in a straight-to-DVD Mary-Kate and Ashley Olsen movie, and is waiting to be *found* is a kind of lunacy. And it puts an awful lot of pressure on you to make the *right* step and get the *right* degree and open the *right* door so the stars align and you can, in a cinematically glorious moment, *Find Your Passion Under the Tuscan Sun.*

I am here to tell you:

You will never *find* your passion and purpose.

There. I said it. You're probably in shock and maybe a little bit angry because you did not splurge on a hardback book only to be given the news that you're never going to find your passion and purpose.

But it's true.

Because your passion and purpose isn't out there, buried like treasure or hiding behind a tree. It's not waiting for you to open the right door or peek under the right rock before it jumps out at you like you're playing some cosmically cruel game of hide-and-seek.

Passion and purpose are not an object of desire or hidden treasure waiting to be *discovered.* They are a canvas that is waiting for you to get the first splatter of paint on it. They are a blank computer screen that needs about 100,000 words on it to make a story, but (because of math and stuff) you can't have 100,000 until you have 10,000 and you can't have 10,000 before you write the first word.

Passion isn't a preexisting condition.

A life of purpose and passion can't be *found.* It is the result of being brave, curious, and dare I say, plucky?

You do not *find* your passion and purpose.

You *build* it.

You start construction when you follow rabbit trails and step forward in the general direction of north. When you ask hard questions of yourself and of the world and when you're brave enough to actually listen to the answer, pivot when necessary, and then *commit.* Even when the glitter and the adrenaline wear off and everyone else moves on to the next shiny thing.

There is no secret. There is no silver bullet. You just have to be brave enough to listen to the whisper that says, "Keep going."

Dave Evans and Bill Burnett, professors at Stanford and founders of the Life Design Lab, have profoundly influenced my belief in the mindset shift from "finding" to "building" our passions.

A series of studies conducted at the Stanford Center on Adolescence found that 8 out of 10 people say they haven't "found their passion" and don't have a clear vision for where they want to go in life.

If you're someone who's been there, who feels like they can't answer that question with absolute clarity and fervor, *you're not alone.* And if not being able to answer that seems to send you into a tailspin of insecurity and anxiety, Evans and Burnett suggest that maybe *you're* not actually the problem.

Maybe the *real* problem is that we're simply asking the wrong question.

What if . . .

Instead of asking what we are *passionate* about, we simply asked, What am I *interested* in?

The stakes are a whole lot lower. The freedom to explore what you're simply *interested in* might create space that allows you to just keep exploring.

There is a wonderful quote by Frederick Buechner, whose work I love dearly, that says, "The place God calls you to is the place where your deep gladness and the world's deep hunger meet."[1]

While I could not agree more with Buechner's sentiment, I would really appreciate it if people stopped using this quote as *instructions* to help you "find your passion." Because this sentiment is more helpful as *a reflection* with the benefit of hindsight than it is to guide you and propel you forward in your journey. After all, the admonishment to go out and "find" the place where our deep gladness and the world's deep hunger meet is quite a tall and intimidating order. We can't actually see that sacred intersection *until we are there.* And if we are not willing start moving forward before we "find it," we'll never make it.

Passion and *Purpose* are built over time with consistency and courage and commitment and pluck.

Interest will suffice for now.

It's in the simple work of being interested and the brave work of exploring and the sacred work of trying and failing and trying again where passion and purpose are not found, but *built.*

Brick by brick, step by step. In our vocations. In our communities. In our families. In ourselves.

It's not for you to "discover" or "find" the straight and narrow path of passion that you can see extend into the future. If you can see the path, if it's relatively straight and narrow, if you have a pretty good idea about how the story ends, then it's *not your story.*

As Antonio Machado reminds us, "Traveler, there is no path. The path is made by walking."[2]

So, Travelers: Let's get moving, shall we?

❊ ❊ ❊

Perhaps even worse than the notion that *the* path that will lead us to our purpose that's waiting to be "discovered" is the idea that we are born with our passion already fully formed within us.

I remember *so distinctly* being in a season of life where I listened to interesting people tell their fascinating life stories, and a phrase like "I've *always* been passionate about . . ." could send me in a tailspin of absolute existential dread and despair. You've *always been passionate* about that?! Like, *always?* Since you were a teen or a kid or in utero or . . . ?

What does that even mean, I've *always been passionate?! Give me the details!!*

Because *my* earliest memory was learning how to ride a bike and flying down a hill and getting clotheslined by a mailbox. Then I remember getting stuck in the laundry chute during a babysitter-(un)supervised game of hide-and-seek. And then I skip like ten years of childhood memories and suddenly recall watching John Travolta in *Phenomenon* and spending an inordinate amount of time lying on my bedroom floor trying to make objects move with my mind in an attempt to figure out how to do my chores without actually moving my body.

And that's basically it, folks. That's all I've got in my "Always since the beginning of time" memory bank that could bolster my claim that I've *always been passionate about something.*

And here is the worst part: this is why you could rightfully call me a hypocritical, chief-of-sinners, con-artist FRAUD.

Until fairly recently, while speaking on stage in front of thousands of people, I would ever so casually say, "I have always been *passionate* about issues facing women and girls living in extreme poverty."

I CONFESS.

And reader, I feel genuinely *bad* about it. Because that statement just isn't true. At best, it was careless, ambiguous, and hyperbolic. At worst, it was a lie that might have accidentally sent someone like my younger self into a bit of an existential tailspin.

The truth is, I did not, in fact, come out of my mother's womb passionate about women and girls living in extreme poverty.

Maya Angelou says, "Do the best you can until you know better. Then when you know better, do better."[3] So, in an attempt to do better, I'm not going to keeping casually spouting lies and telling people that I was *always passionate* about these issues. Instead, I'll tell you the actual, less-catchy and not-as-sexy truth: at some point, I started to *slowly* grow increasingly *interested and intrigued* by issues that were facing women and girls across the globe.

My passion for using entrepreneurship to create educational, economic, and leadership opportunities for women who will then go on to be pioneers for gender equality and economic justice started as no more than a nagging sense that if I just kept asking questions and following leads, I'd confirm my suspicion that the world is not as it should be. That there is work to be done.

And that quiet and small interest lead to a subtle but growing desire to have some part in creating a future that is a little bit better and brighter for women and girls everywhere.

That's it.

I did not come into the world with a burning passion inside me. And I did not drink some Magical Millennial Potion before bed and wake up the next morning having "found my passion."

After the revelation that I had been unintentionally lying about my story,* I spent a lot of time noodling on this and

*If you came to hear me speak before about 2015, you're welcome to submit a ticket for a full refund at LizIsALiar.com.

trying to figure out where exactly the first tiny inkling of this *interest* of mine appeared. I parsed it out even further and tried to figure out when I first became conscious and aware of the way gender profoundly influences our individual experiences and eventually how that same dynamic governs many of the structures and policies that dictate how the world works.

After taking a few walks down memory lane, I was able to identify the first time I felt it. *It* being this acute awareness that how the world saw me was, in ways I couldn't yet articulate, influenced profoundly by the fact that I was *a girl.* It wasn't big. It wasn't loud. It would make a terribly boring movie. It was a simple moment in time. A whisper, really.

But Traveler, building a life of purpose and passion is not about waiting for a Loud Call. It's about getting better at listening to the whispers, the inklings, and the hunches.

For me, the first whisper I can remember happened in middle school. As a bright-eyed 13-year-old, I learned about the epic tradition of the annual Lip Sync competition that was the headlining event of "Spirit Week" and the pinnacle of life as I knew it. I literally felt like I died and went to nerdy-theatre-kid heaven.

Never before in the history of our school had the eighth graders won the Lip Sync competition against the upperclassmen. But I was determined to change this. I had found my raison d'etre. I ran a tight ship and held practices every night of the week leading up to our grand performance.

One night, a few days before the show, I was demonstrating how to do *the perfect* jazz square while narrating the instructions through a bullhorn I found in the athletics closet when

Neil Ferguson* yelled, "Listen up, everybody! The *Femi-Nazi* has something to say!" and stood at attention with an index finger faux mustache and a Hitler-esque raised hand pointed in my direction. A group of my fellow students *erupted* in laughter and a charming nickname that followed me for many years was born.

Femi-Nazi.

I hadn't ever heard this phrase before, but I had read *The Diary of Anne Frank* and knew enough to know that Nazi wasn't a compliment. And the "Femi" preposition led me to believe it had *something* to do with me being a girl.

But yet, I watched as Neil himself was praised on the football field and hailed as "a leader" for using the same passion (and volume) to shout commands at his fellow athletes that I used to direct my fellow Lip-Syncers.

The message was loud and clear: what this young man needed was some guidance and coaching on how to hone and optimize his natural leadership gifts. What *I* needed, on the other hand, was a good bout of public shaming to encourage me to sit down, settle down, quiet down, and simmer down.

Down,

down,

down.

It was loud and clear.

From that moment on, when I would speak up in class or get a little fired up about something, I knew I ran the risk of hearing someone snicker or call out "Femi-Nazi!" which, even

*Name changed to protect the little jerk. Just kidding. It's his real name! Let's send him thousands of tampons in the mail with notes that say "I'm Not Bossy, I'm the Boss!" OK. Update: my publisher's legal department nixed this idea. #FunPolice

though I didn't want to admit it, made me think twice before speaking my mind.

This experience led to an increasing awareness of the role that gender plays in how I saw myself and how others saw me, and how I was both rewarded or penalized for my behavior through the lens of gender. No passion per say, just interest and awareness.

Having grown up in the Midwest, I had BIG DREAMS and aspirations of attending college in some exotic, non-landlocked locale. But the day after I graduated from high school, my parents announced they were divorcing, and at the last minute, I decided to stay closer to the home that seemed to be crumbling before my very eyes. I had worked hard in high school toward collegiate fantasies of a private school with a manicured campus dotted with old brick buildings, and small class sizes where students were regularly invited to dinners with their professors and fellow classmates. Instead, I'd be attending a huge state school with 30,000 of my closest pals just over an hour from my hometown, which was both a huge disappointment and, frankly, a blow to my ego given all my lofty talk about getting out of Dodge. Largely in order to salvage my pride, I chose to major in journalism, not necessarily because I had a fiery passion for reporting but because the University of Missouri has one of the best journalism schools in the entire country, and I figured that if I had to stay in Missouri, I might as well get the most bang for my diploma buck and choose the school's specialty. While making the decisions I was taught to believe would set the trajectory for my entire future, I didn't feel "fueled by passion," and it certainly wasn't a fulfillment of the dreams I had worked hard toward.

It honestly felt more like very pragmatically trying to make the most of the less-than-ideal circumstances I found myself in during that confusing and turbulent season of life.*

During college, my vague interest in issues facing women and girls slowly, and in the most undramatic way possible, started to grow. I took some classes, worked for a campus publication that covered domestic and international human rights issues, and occasionally volunteered for nonprofits or participated in campaigns happening around campus. And in the simple act of showing up at the rally or volunteering at the shelter, I eventually started asking some very difficult questions about some Very Big Problems that went way beyond me and my humiliating middle school moments. Problems like global extreme poverty, domestic violence, human trafficking, rape as a weapon of war, and why these atrocities disproportionately affect women and girls.

But *even still*, if you would have pulled me aside and asked me what I was *passionate* about, I am almost positive I would not have been able to answer you. It didn't feel like I had found the "passion" I was on the hunt for.

Just interest and intrigue.

Today, over ten years later, I can look back and say that I never did find my passion or purpose.

But I am *building* it.

---

*In hindsight I can easily see that there was immense blessing in what felt like only disappointment at the time. I was able to graduate from this in-state, public school debt free with degrees I am truly very proud of. I feel confident that had I emerged from the private college I was planning to attend, saddled with a *massive* amount of student debt, there is a good chance my story would be very different. I've come to believe that the student debt crisis in this country is one of the biggest impediments to entrepreneurship and innovation.

Perhaps, above all else, the most important mindset shift you'll make in the Beginner's Pluck journey is to understand the difference between *finding* and *building*.

The critical difference is this: when you set out to "find" something, it requires that you know what you're looking for. When we believe in the notion that we will eventually "find" our purpose and passion, we bide our time, living only half alive and gripped by fear. We look to others who have already "found it," and we get jealous, overwhelmed, and confused when we try to run someone else's race because we want to end up where they are.

We cling to this narrative of "finding" because it is self-soothing and gives us permission to be passive, and we fall asleep to the world and to the work that is right in front of us.

We can blame our lack of direction and purpose on The Universe and Other Vague External Factors instead of taking responsibility for our own lives and moving forward with courage and intentionality.

When we believe our passion and purpose is waiting to be found, we wait instead of *create*.

The mentality around creating and building is much different than finding or discovering. Have you ever heard an author describe the process of writing the novel without knowing how the story ends? They don't talk about the moment when they *finally found* the perfect last sentence which then gave them permission to start writing. They talk about how each day, they sit down with an openness to where the narrative will go, and they know *they* must write it into existence. In the end, they sit back and marvel not at their *discovery*, but at their *creation*.

Your passion isn't found in your dreaming. It's *made* by your *doing*.

There is no *aha!*

There is no secret.

But there is moving.

And there is doing.

There is exploring and creating and building and deconstructing and reconstructing. And the more open you are to exploration, the more empowered and free and energized you will become to be a builder and creator of a life of purpose and passion.

So Travelers, before we continue, I will ask you to, at least temporarily, lay aside the visions of grandeur you've had of what it will look like when you finally strike gold and "*find your passion*" so we can get down to the business of learning how *to build it*.

THREE

Dream Small

I'm planning a nationwide covert operation. Will you join me? It involves wearing all black and accessing your inner Russian Spy Alter Ego. (You can call me Nadia.*) On the fourth night of the full moon we shall convene at our local high schools and when the clock strikes midnight, we will enter into these facilities and destroy all posters with the words DREAM BIG accompanied by images of astronauts and bald eagles and . . . sports things.

Will you join me on this mission? (They say that a good friend bails you out of jail. A *great* friend says to you from the cell across the way, "Well, that was fun!")

Now, don't get me wrong. Despite my facetious† call to vandalism, I am absolutely a big fan of Big Dreams. The best compliment I have ever been given in my life was by someone

---

*Siri calls me Nadia Gorbachev. If you want to spice up your days and make them feel a little more adventurous, just have Siri call you by your alter ego.

†The publisher's legal department insisted I clarify. Geez. Chapter three and I've already gotten in trouble twice with Legal.

who told me that by hanging out with me, they were brain-washed into believing they could achieve their biggest, wildest dreams. In fact, this entire book is to actually help get you to a place where you are Dreaming (and doing!) Bigger than you ever have before.

However, from my experience, Dreaming BIG is not always the best or most helpful place to *start*. And if you're on a mission to build a life of purpose and passion, you've got to start somewhere.

And that somewhere, Pluckies, can be small.

So, in direct opposition to every inspirational leadership guru you follow on Instagram telling you on a near-daily basis to Dream Big, I'm going to tell you . . .

Go ahead and
dream small!

* * *

I finished my undergrad early and scored a research position in the global studies department of the journalism school that allowed me to earn a (virtually free) master's degree and still graduate with most of my friends. But when grad school graduation (and subsequently the threat of bills and health insurance) started to loom large and it became increasingly obvious that a steady income would be a necessary part of non-academia adulting, I applied for approximately 10,000 jobs. From a staff journalist position at a dinky newspaper in Iowa to an opening at the *New York Times*. I sent resumes to various nonprofits, think tanks, and social justice advocacy organizations. (There was also a wild, semi-desperate night when I applied to be an NBC page at *The Tonight Show*.) I got a handful of interviews and one or two very *meh* job offers, but nothing that *remotely* felt like it fulfilled my God-given right as a recent, idealistic, American college graduate to land My Dream Job.

But bills are bills so I took the best offer on the table and went to work at the lowest possible level for a highly regarded global communications firm in my hometown. It was a far cry from my dream job, but worry you not, I had a Big Change the World dream to keep me warm at night.

My Big Dream was a vision for a corporate philanthropy initiative that involved millions of dollars and was going to improve the lives of millions of women and girls across the globe. It was a REALLY BIG DREAM, you guys. So many zeros. So many lives. Just you wait! This was going to be *BIG*.

In the meantime, day after day, I went to my job where I compiled media reports and wrote pitches and hosted focus groups for big corporations trying to get bigger. When I'd actually allow myself to be honest, I felt very little purpose in my work. But each morning I'd quell those feelings by comforting myself with this vague notion that I could just keep walking down the path I was on, slowly advancing enough through the corporate ranks, until someday when maybe I would finally have the power to call the shots and I could manifest my BIG DREAM that would give my life purpose and meaning. That Big Fancy Someday Dream helped numb me to the growing suspicion that this stable and impressive-looking path I was on was not actually the path *I* was made for walking.

And then one day, sitting in my cubicle on the 18th floor, everything changed.

I was doing some research for a client when I stumbled across a little video called *The Girl Effect*. The video starts by bemoaning the BIG PROBLEMS in the world: Poverty, AIDS,

Hunger, War. And then it proposes that perhaps the solution to all of it is investing in *a girl*.[1]

There is a brief, two-second frame where the only word on an otherwise black screen is the word GIRL, representing one, single girl. And because it was only text with no visual to accompany it, I subconsciously started scouring my brain for the face of ONE GIRL to visualize this point that I already agreed with.

ONE GIRL who grew up in extreme poverty and had unjustly and inexplicably been forced to shoulder the burden of the world's Big Problems.

And you know what?

In that split second, I couldn't conjure up an image of a single, real girl who I *actually knew*.

And it stopped me dead in my idealistic, Grand Plan, Big Dream, someday-I-am-going-to-help-bring-A-MILLION-GIRLS-out-of-poverty tracks.

I'd happily donate what I could to a cause or show up to a march or post the relevant hashtag on social media, but the actual life that I was building, there on the 18th floor of this global communications firm, was entirely unaffected by the economic realities facing billions of women.

While I was busy thinking and dreaming and scheming about a million girls, the sacred importance and value of just one got lost somewhere along the way. With tears streaming down my face, I realized there was quite a delta between what I *said* I cared about and the life I was building.

My friendships.

My community.

My story.

With an honest evaluation, it was obvious that *my* story still had a neat and sturdy wall around it that allowed me to engage intellectually in The Issues and The Cause while keeping me safely in my own little reality. These walls allowed me the luxury of choosing just when and where and how I would allow my story to be affected by *hers*.

Having this choice in the first place is called privilege.* And privilege is what allowed me (and still does and *always* will, although I hope to a lesser extent today than it did back then) to build a life with a remarkably convenient ON/OFF switch. I could engage with The Issues when it worked for me. When *I* had the time, the capacity, the desire. But there was no relationship or community.

After having this split-second realization that I didn't have a relationship with a single girl who grew up in extreme poverty, I traded in my Grand Plan and my Big Dreams that I held in my back pocket for "someday"—and my focus shifted entirely.

*Perhaps now would be a good time to make it abundantly clear, if it's not already, that this book is written from a position and perspective of extreme privilege. They say to write what you know, so here I am writing *my story* from the vantage point of the privilege that I am still working to fully unpack and understand today. The night before I left for Uganda, I had what I would call a prophetic dream that profoundly impacted me, not just during my time in Uganda but in the decade since. The gist of the dream was this: I was in an unfamiliar place and some terrible, dangerous tragedy broke out. I was experiencing all the fear and terror that everyone around me was facing when a helicopter came and rescued me. I resisted the rescue and pleaded with them to let me bring others along. However, they said they didn't have room and they grabbed me and put me into the helicopter. As the helicopter rose above the chaos, I was crying and pleading for them to go back for the others, feeling guilty and horrified for my friends who were left behind. However, I was also grateful and relieved that *I* had a way out. That dream was a profound and harsh realization of the reality of the world we live in and the space I occupy as a privileged, white American. Although I can choose to, as activist Brittany Packnett would say, "spend my privilege" in a way that I hope will create pathways and platforms for those who have less privilege than me, it's important to acknowledge that I will never, ever experience the world in the way they do. Simply by nature of where I was born and the color of my skin, I will never be left behind, forgotten, and marginalized in the way many others, in our own country and across the world, systematically are. This dream is as clear to me today as it was the night I had it. It both sobers and motivates me, in a way that only the truest dreams can.

In that very moment, against every ounce of my Millennial-minded, Big Dreaming self, I started . . .

Dreaming Small.

Really small, in fact.

Remember that scene in *Honey, I Shrunk the Kids* when Wayne Szalinski's kids get accidentally shrunk to a quarter-inch tall? Well, you could say my Big Dreams got *Szalinskied.*

My new dream became not landing my Dream Job or bringing a million girls out of poverty, but rather, simply closing the gap between what I said I cared about and my actual day-to-day life. I wanted to make friends. I wanted to build a community that would reflect my desire to be a co-creator in a world that is a little bit bigger and brighter and more just than the one I was currently occupying. I wanted to learn, not just from facts and figures and articles and documentaries, but in real life, on the ground, from those who were experiencing the issues and challenges I said I cared about. I wanted my story to be tied up with hers in a way that was messy and broken and beautiful *and small.*

I wanted to know just

One girl.

That was the new, microscopically small dream. Meet and become actual friends with *one* girl. I needed zero degrees. Zero connections. Zero fancy job titles. Zero million-dollar budgets. Zero strategic plans. And zero people to give me permission.

Which all, of course, meant *zero* excuses.

That Big Dream I held in my back pocket for *someday* may have sounded impressive, but it did not compel me to make any *real* moves. And let's be very clear that planning and dreaming is not the same as moving and actually doing. As Bob Goff says, "No one will be remembered for what they just *planned* to do."[2]

But you know what happened within *hours* of (temporarily) giving up the Someday Big Dream and instead (accidentally) dreaming really, really small?

I became a Doer instead of just a Dreamer.

I made a move.

My first move.

A big move, at that.

A big, not-well-thought-out, kind-of-impulsive move. Sometimes, the small dreams are what propel us toward actually making a move. Big or small moves, it doesn't actually matter. What matters is that you know that movement is your lifeline. And if a small dream is what fuels the movement, then small dreams win.

Every time.

I exchanged a few emails with a friend from college who had moved to Uganda a few years earlier, and then I opened up a new tab on my desktop computer and went to Kayak. com and bought myself a one-way ticket to Entebbe, Uganda.

The extent of my knowledge of Uganda was mostly limited to a Peace & Conflict Resolution class I took in undergrad where I wrote a paper about the Lord's Resistance Army and the two-decade-long civil conflict in Northern Uganda. During this conflict, children were kidnapped—the boys forced into war and girls into sex slavery for the rebel army group.

If my new goal in life was to make *one friend* and learn more, firsthand, about the realities facing girls growing up in extreme poverty and conflict zones, Uganda seemed like a fine place to do just that.

Dreaming that teensy, unimpressive Small Dream of meeting one girl got me *real good.*

That's just how powerful Small Dreams can be. When you finally have the freedom to Dream Small, you're no longer under the weight of either the Big Dream itself or the pressure you feel to even have a Big Dream in the first place, which creates a little bit of breathing room for the Small Dream that might have been waiting patiently all along to be seen and heard and taken seriously.

My Big Dream sounded really impressive but didn't do a darn thing for propelling me out of the Dreaming and into the Doing. That Big Dream lulled me into contentment by convincing me that the only thing I could do was wait. Wait until I got promoted. Wait until I had more power and respect. Wait until I knew more Important People. Wait until I had more access to resources. Wait until I had proved myself. Oh, the dream was big, but it didn't move me. Not one inch.

Finding excuses to keep you from taking the first step toward your Big Dream is deliriously easy. There are so many! Maybe you find yourself humming the tune that goes something like, "It's not the right time. I'm not financially stable enough. I need to be a little more confident. I need one more connection. I need one more year of experience. I need permission and affirmation from my mother and my brother and my husband and the lady who bags my groceries while I'm at it."

But when you finally let a Small Dream take up the sacred space it actually deserves?

Excuses are much harder to come by.

There are lots of excuses that can keep you from pursuing your Big Dream of quitting your job and becoming a full-time artist who can actually pay their bills and then some. So, make it smaller. Go smaller and smaller until you have no more excuses. Dream Small about selling your very first art piece. Just one. What will it feel like? What will you do with your earnings? Who is the first person you'll tell? If you really want it, there are not a lot of excuses that can keep you from hopping on Etsy and setting up shop (this should take less time than it takes to watch two episodes of *The Office*). Next up? Send an email to your 25 closest acquaintances and tell them you're open for business. See what happens. Keep going.

There are so many reasons you could come up with for why you could never start an organization that fundamentally transforms how your state addresses homelessness. So, make it smaller. Dream Small about having a real and meaningful relationship with a fellow human who has experienced homelessness firsthand. Think about what it will feel like to have your worldview broadened by the experience of *a friend*. Think about how you'll feel knowing that you're taking an active step toward co-creating even just a tiny corner of the universe that is warm and safe and dignified for a human who deserves no less. If you really want it, there is absolutely no reason why you can't invite Perry, the man on the corner of Stark St. and 82nd, over for dinner next Tuesday night. Next up? Ask Perry to bring a friend to dinner the following Tuesday night. See what happens. Keep going.

Now, if you're already dreaming Big Dreams and that Big Dream is compelling you on a daily basis toward the actions and steps you need to take to get you there, go you! We're rooting for you! But if, whether you're on the starting block or at a crossroads, you're feeling stuck or scared or overwhelmed, don't do *anything else* before you give yourself permission to Dream Small.

Small Dreams matter, Traveler. I will forever champion your Small Dreams because I know the surprising power they hold in catapulting us out of waiting and into creating. And they may be the very thing that sets your dream into the motion of doing.

After all, it was a tiny, unimpressive, half-baked Small Dream of simply knowing *one girl* that was responsible for pushing me from a state of paralyzed Big Dreaming into actually *doing* and then, get this, eventually Dreaming Big again. But make no mistake, dreaming remarkably, microscopically *small* was my first real step toward not finding but *building* a life of purpose and impact.

FOUR

Choose Curiosity over Criticism

When I told my parents that I had quit my job to move to Uganda by myself with zero plan, they had the audacity to ask *why*. When I told them basically I was going to make friends, you can imagine their horror/shock/confusion.

"To make friends?" they said. "Can't you just join a running club like your sister?* What exactly are you going to *do*? What is *the plan*?"

In slight defense of their aghast, I should say that I wasn't particularly well-traveled, and certainly had never moved to a place that may well have been Mars to them. And me too.

Over the last several years, I've met many remarkable, wordly people who grew up in globe-trotting families. They got their first passport virtually at birth and speak a few

---

*Obviously, they did not remember my first gymnastics meet and subsequent athletic career NEARLY as clearly as I did. LUCKY THEM.

languages and casually refer to their family friends in various parts of the world.

Just to be clear, this was *not* my family.

We vacationed mainly to places our Ford Windstar minivan (dubbed the White Wonder) would take us. We spent spring breaks and summer vacations at the Lake of the Ozarks in Missouri, and if we got really crazy, we'd road trip to Destin, Florida, and spend our allowance on lower-back henna tattoos and T-shirts with our faces airbrushed on them.

I got my first passport at 18 when I took a Senior Trip with my best friends and our moms and really cut my world-traveler teeth . . . .

At an all-inclusive resort in Puerto Vallarta where *thankfully* we never needed to venture off the hotel property.

I was very cultured, you guys.

There was nothing about our family history or my background or experience that would lead my parents to believe that "Moving to Uganda Without a Plan" would be a successful endeavor. When it came to cross-cultural, global solo-adventures, it would be quite fair and accurate to label me a Beginner.

Once I arrived in Uganda, a friend from college agreed to pick me up at the airport, but she was over two hours late. My flight landed at 11 PM, so at around 1 AM, I was sitting in a nearly deserted airport an hour outside of the capital city. I had no phone. No address. No Plan B for if my ride never showed up. I told approximately 3,456 taxi drivers who approached me asking if I needed a ride, as confidently as I could muster, "Thanks but no thanks! My friend Kristen will be here any minute!"

Kristen eventually showed up, and my life in Uganda began. Turns out, everything I had learned out of books and documentaries about Uganda proved to be true. But, as so often Westerners tend to do with Africa, I had formed what Chimamanda Ngozi Adichie calls "a single story" about Africa and about what life in Uganda would look like.[1]

I, embarrassingly, had *zero* concept that in addition to mud huts and refugee camps and infamous war lords, Uganda had a capital city of two million people and had fancy hotels and tall buildings and a fantastic international food scene where I would fall in love with chicken tikka masala for the first time.

However, before my trip, with images of mud huts and wild warthogs in mind, I headed to the annual REI used gear sale and left outfitted like a woman who would be living in the bush for a few years. I was ready for my Grand Adventure with a hiking pack, headlamp, some dehydrated packets of food (you know, that people take to THE MOON and such), and a single-person tent.

Imagine my surprise when on *night two* of being in Uganda, I met a new group of friends who took me to a bumpin' night club filled with the most beautiful, well-dressed Ugandans you could possibly imagine. I had managed to make it through early adulthood never having stepped foot in a nightclub, but my rule for the trip was to Say Yes to Adventure. (That and I had no other friends and exactly *zero* other compelling offers for how to spend my first Friday night in town.) So, here I was in my long, dusty hippy-girl skirt, a pair of muddy Chaco sandals, and my Mountainsmith day pack trying *real hard* to be cool when in reality I was NOT COOL AT ALL EVEN A LITTLE BIT. I looked like a Duggar who had wandered off the set of *19 Kids and Counting* and into a club that could have been in a trendy neighborhood in Brooklyn.

While people were standing around the bar to get cocktails like normal good-looking, well-dressed young adults with friends, I was all like, "Hey guys! Anyone need a sip of my iodine purified water I'm carrying around in my new CamelBak water apparatus mainly worn by people climbing Mt. Everest and *completely* inappropriate and humiliating for the night club context we're in right now? No? OK, cool."

In all my thinking and dreaming and researching and writing about the effects of extreme poverty on women and girls, I didn't assume that *of course* Uganda would be a complex and multifaceted landscape. Night clubs alongside slums. Beautiful, gated homes with lush palm tree landscaping, where just outside, a destitute mama sits with her head hung low and a hungry baby in her lap. Not all that unlike walking past the Louis Vuitton store in downtown Chicago and bumping into a strung-out veteran begging for money on the very same corner. Complex dichotomies *here* and *there*. Go figure.

But I was caught off guard by this. And *embarrassed* and a little confused, if I'm being honest. This trip was not at all turning out to be what I had envisioned.

✳ ✳ ✳

In these inevitable moments of feeling embarrassed or confused or discouraged, you've got an incredibly important decision to make: you can choose criticism and let the Spiral of Shame continue down its dark and twisty path. Or, you can harness your Inner Beginner and *choose curiosity*.

You can aim that criticism outward, which means you respond to feelings of failure, frustration, or incompetency by blaming your surroundings or circumstances: "If only *he* would listen better. If only *she* wasn't so self-centered. If only my school had a better job placement program. If only I had more connections. If only *they* weren't so stuck in their old ways, they'd love my great, new idea for the business." External criticism will leave you in a cynical, responsibility-evading paralysis.

Or you turn the blame on yourself: "I'm such an idiot. Who do I think I am? If only I were smart enough/good-looking enough/likeable enough/outgoing enough/creative enough this wouldn't have happened. I better give up now before everyone catches on to what a screw-up loser I really am." Internal criticism will lead you to a self-pity party of death.

You can choose criticism

or

you can, in moments of challenge, disappointment, failure, confusion, and embarrassment decide to *choose* a spirit of curiosity.

It's one or the other.

Every time.

Instead of finding someone and something to blame, you can start to ask yourself some questions: "I wonder why they responded that way? What could I have done better? What will I do differently next time? How will I learn/change/grow from this experience? What else might I be missing here? How can I get a fuller understanding of the situation?"

Curiosity is not only one of the greatest tools we have in building lives of purpose and passion, it's a mindset that each and every one of us can choose, each and every day. And in doing so, you can build up your curiosity muscle. Curiosity is there, right in front of you, in unlimited quantity. And the reason I know this is because each and every one of us was born with a remarkable and divine sense of curiosity.

Curiosity may perhaps be the most consistent and defining characteristic of childhood. Before a kid can walk and talk, they are constantly putting things in their mouths in an attempt to learn and understand as much of the world around them with the limited resources they have.

My son is two years old and we are in a full-on season of "But *why*?" Just a few days ago, after his helium balloon flew away, he asked "Why?" SEVENTEEN THOUSAND times in a row, drilling down so far into his inquiry that after a rather pathetic explanation of the difference in weight between Helium and Oxygen, I finally had to simply end The Toddler Inquisition with an exasperated, "Because, I don't know, that's the way God made the molecules." He wanted to know why that balloon floated away and there was no shame, no filter, just his natural posture of taking in the world for the first time and then asking *why, why*, yeah but, *whyyyyyyy?*

What's remarkable about the journey and commitment to become more curious is that curiosity isn't something you have to "achieve." It's simply a place you have to find your way back to. Whether you're just starting out or well on your way to becoming an expert, curiosity is the art of becoming fully awake once again.

✳ ✳ ✳

Curiosity will not only help you take those first, daunting steps, but will actually make you *more successful in the long run* at whatever it is you choose to build and create.

And you don't just have to take my word for it. In fact, there are legitimate lab-coat-wearing social scientists who have graciously done the work to prove this little theory that curiosity makes us more successful.

Researchers at the University of Illinois Urbana-Champaign and Southern Mississippi University asked two groups of people to solve the exact same set of puzzles. All conditions were the same except for *one*. With one group of participants, they were asked to spend one minute prior to starting the exercise telling themselves: "I will succeed!"

The second group was asked to spend one minute prior to the test *asking questions* and wondering if they in fact would solve the puzzles. Instead of saying "I will," they asked, "*Will I?*"

And guess what!

The folks in Group Two, who asked questions before attempting to solve the puzzle, outperformed those in Group One, who said declaratively, "I will!" by a whopping 50 percent!

I agree with the scientists, who conclude that "research like this challenges traditional paradigms regarding public service messages and self-help literature designed to motivate people toward healthier or more productive behavior."[2]

Now, I am all for power posing and positive self-talk. It's obviously a far greater alternative than negative self-talk. If "Self, you are awesome!" gives you a boost of energy and confidence in the morning or before a big meeting or a hard conversation *go for it.*

BUT if you *really* want to game the system and increase your likelihood of success, stand in front of the mirror and, not out of negative or demeaning self-doubt, but out of a spirit of genuine curiosity, ask yourself: Will I?

Will I be the most patient and present parent I can be today?

Will I make this the best client presentation I've ever
  given?

Will I be honest and true to my feelings but stay in control of my emotions when I have this hard conversation I'm dreading?

Will I be brave enough to ask for the promotion and
  confident and articulate when I explain why I believe I
  deserve it?

You're more likely to be successful the moment you *choose
curiosity*, and here's why: when we use *questions* instead of declarative statements, it puts us in a posture of openness where
we're ready to actually learn, grow, and change. By simply
asking the question, you're giving a clue to your brain that it's
very possible you don't have it all figured out just quite yet *and
that's okay.* You're starting to use self-talk and language that
normalizes and de-shames the prospect that you have room
to grow. You're giving yourself permission to start creatively
problem-solving, making new connections and generating
ideas that will lead you to the most effective possible solutions.

Furthermore, as Daniel Pink explains in his book *To Sell Is
Human*, "the interrogative, by its very form elicits answers—
and within those answers are strategies for actually carrying
out the task."[3] Questions elicit a *response* in a way that even
the most positive declarative statements just don't. Join me in
a little make-believe to help illustrate this point.

Let's pretend I am getting ready to walk into a meeting
with a potential investor. And let's say that the morning of
my big meeting I stand in front of my bathroom mirror and
put my hands on my hips in a power stance and say to myself,

"Liz! You're *AMAZING*! You're the most awesome CEO and smartest entrepreneur there ever was! You're going to *rock* this meeting!"

OK. That's a nice sentiment. But my positive self-talk ends there with an elusive, hyperbolic statement of my awesomeness that I may or may not actually really believe.

But, let's say before that very same meeting I simply ask myself, "Why will this be the *best* pitch I've ever given?" The question elicits a response. And my response in this scenario might go something like this:

> Well, the last time I gave this pitch, I realized that I wasn't really reading my audience as well as I could have been. I spent too much time talking about our mission and ran out of time to really dive into our potential for growth and answer the investor's questions about financing our inventory. So, this time, I am going to set the timer on my phone so that I can glance down and be more aware of time and make sure I can give a more well-rounded picture of our entire business.

Now will this be a great pitch? Yeah!

By asking a simple question, I started a rich and productive train of thought that gave me permission to acknowledge that I have room to grow. The response pulled from prior experiences, inspired an actual action step for making it better, and left me feeling totally empowered and equipped to succeed.

But it gets even better: asking yourself questions also taps into your **why**. Your truest why and core motivation comes not from what others want or need or expect from you, but instead is from deep within *you*. Questions inspire you to tap into the deepest part of your desires and seriously ask yourself what you want out of life. And not just what you want *now*, but what you want in *the long run*.

Why do I want this to be the best investor pitch I've ever given?

Because we need the capital to implement the new program.

Why do I want to implement the new program?

Because that is how we are going to grow the company.

Why do I want to grow the company?

Because the more we grow, the more we can create dignified opportunities for women in Uganda and Ethiopia and the United States and India to become more of who they were created to be. And then those women will go on to create opportunities for others to do the same. This is the world I want to live in: a world of people in process of becoming who they were created to be and lighting a path of justice and equality and dignity and adventure and wonder for others to join in a global community of Dreamers and Doers. And at this exact moment in time, my tiny role in this Big Beautiful Story involves absolutely crushing this pitch.

That's **why**.

Now will this be the best pitch I've ever given in the history of the universe?

Heck, yes!

* * *

There is also scientific evidence that suggests curiosity is *just as important* as IQ in achieving long-term success. The more curious you are, the more able you are to tolerate ambiguity,[4] navigate complexity, and acquire knowledge[5] over time. Studies have shown that increased curiosity is associated with less-defensive reactions to stress and less-aggressive reactions to provocation. It's incredibly difficult to increase your IQ but you *can* increase your CQ, which stands for Curiosity Quotient.

You can start building up your curiosity muscle *today* by simply asking questions and creating a little space for wonder and surprise. And being smarter, more accomplished, more resourced or networked or successful does not make it easier to be curious. In fact, it arguably makes it more difficult. The more you think you've got the world figured out and the more you have riding on all your fancy plans working out, the harder it is to be truly, un-biasedly, insatiably curious. This is Beginner's Pluck edge. Your advantage. Your head start.

Interesting people with interesting lives are . . . *interested*. And you do not need permission from anyone else to be interested.

Interesting people are curious and interested in how things work. Interested in how to make things better. Interested in others. Interested in stories and experiences. Interested in exploring what would happen if we stopped letting our fears and insecurities scream louder than the heartbreakingly beautiful and haunting and quiet and cacophonous symphony of a life lived freely out of curiosity, conviction, and compassion.

✳ ✳ ✳

Standing there in that nightclub in Uganda, I felt confused and taken aback by my lack of knowledge or understanding and frankly embarrassed by my aimless cluelessness. In these moments of embarrassment and confusion, we are faced with a choice: we can choose criticism and spiral into shame or cynicism *or* we choose to start pumping some serious iron and build up our curiosity muscles.

Every time you choose curiosity over criticism, you're growing your CQ and taking steps toward the truly life-changing magic of being more curious, more successful, and most importantly, more of who you were created to be.

So,

Will you?

INTERLUDE
Gulu, Uganda > London, England > Portland, Oregon

My friend Sister Rosemary may be the Poster Child–Cover Girl–Patron Saint of Beginner's Pluck. If my publisher would have okayed it, *her* face would be on the cover of this book. At a few inches shy of five feet tall, this Nike-sneaker-wearing Ugandan nun has enough pluck to last a lifetime.

Sister Rosemary directs a school called Saint Monica's, and during the height of the conflict in Northern Uganda, she sheltered children who were at risk of being kidnapped by the Lord's Resistance Army. For years and years, every night she stood guard outside the gate of the school, armed against the rebel soldiers only with whispered prayers.

Saint Monica's is a place where girls come to rebuild, to heal and to belong. For girls who were not lucky enough to be protected from the rebel soldiers, it is the place where their broken and bruised bodies and spirits go to mend.

Perhaps what I love most about Sister Rosemary is that she is a *feisty* one. But what's beautiful is that she channels her fire and anger and frustration into action and compassion and curiosity. Sister Rosemary taught me to choose curiosity over criticism.

A few years back, I was walking around Saint Monica's with Sister Rosemary and she was explaining to me that for *years* she was pained by the incessant litter on her property. She felt like she was constantly picking up plastic bottles and bags and soda cans. As she explained her frustration, it was *palpable*. She sounded like an exasperated mom, feeling like her days just consisted of being a glorified janitor, and she was so. over. it. Her spirit of criticism for all the people and circumstances at fault for this out-of-control litter situation was at an all-time high.

Then one day, she read a story online about someone who made an entire house out of plastic bottles. *No kidding,* she thought to herself. She took a breather from her criticism and let her curiosity run amuck. She dove deeper into the story and downloaded YouTube videos and learned as much as she could about plastic bottle architecture.

Fueled by her insatiable curiosity, she learned that a building made from plastic bottles filled with mud is stronger than brick. It is temperature regulated and keeps the interior around 65 degrees, even when the hot Ugandan sun is beating down. It's earthquake- and even bullet-proof.

No kidding.

While cursing the existence of these plastic bottles, she was also fundraising for Saint Monica's. She needed more buildings on the property for the girls and for guests, but she didn't have the funds to build them. And now she didn't need the funds. Because she had bottles.

Bottles on bottles on bottles.

Those bottles started out as the bane of her existence. But with a dose insatiable curiosity, they became her treasure in disguise.

After (gently) shoving me into one of her bottle houses so I could experience the nice, cool temperature for myself, Sister Rosemary let out a guttural laugh. "Every time I used to see another stupid bottle on my property I got angry and asked WHY? Now, I see those bottles and I say, 'Weeeeeee! Thank you, Jesus, for more trash!'"

Sister Rosemary now has a mini-village of beautiful little houses made from garbage.

If, like Sister Rosemary, we want to build a life of purpose and impact, we've got to learn how to channel our confusion, embarrassment, or frustration into *curiosity*.

WWSRD?

(What Would Sister Rosemary Do?)

FIVE

Be on Assignment in Your Own Life

Several weeks after the night club incident, I was still mostly aimless, jobless, and friendless, and my insecurities about having no plan and nothing to offer were mounting. One day, I was walking down a sidewalk in Kampala to who-knows-where,* as one who is trying to make friends does. Cars were zooming down the adjacent main road. Just as I happened to look up, I saw a man dart across the busy road and get hit by an SUV that didn't slow down even a little bit before the impact. His body flew into the air and he came down on the windshield of the truck only to bounce off and land in the grassy median like a lifeless rag doll. I had never seen anything like this in real life and automatically assumed that I had just witnessed a death.

---

*OK. I actually remember *exactly* where I was going. I was going to the little frozen yogurt and pizza place near the Bukoto Roundabout. I just didn't want admit that in the midst of my floundering, friend-finding loserdom, I was regularly comforting myself with pizza and fro-yo.

I was terrified.

My heart was racing, and in a moment of sheer terror, I looked around for help and realized that I was much closer to the man than anyone else. I obviously couldn't just keep walking or stand there and wait for someone else to help, so as soon as there was a gap in the traffic, I darted across the street and knelt down next to the man without a clue of what I could actually do.

To my complete and utter surprise, he opened his eyes! And then sat upright!

Out of sheer shock, I just blurted out the first thing that came to mind, which was, "Are you okay?!" and the man looked at me, with blood running down his forehead and said to me, completely *deadpan*: "No, I am not OKAY. I just got hit by a car. I need to go to the hospital."

To which I had to reply in so many words: *Well sir, I have neither a cell phone nor a car nor an understanding of the local language nor the faintest idea of where a hospital might be nor any medical knowledge that extends beyond the first two seasons of* Grey's Anatomy, *so I feel like you're really out of luck with me as your guardian angel first responder.*

As he looked up at me with a mix of understandable frustration and disdain, a rush of Ugandans made it onto the scene and (rightfully) shooed me away so they could, you know, actually *be helpful.*

And this was the straw that broke the camel's back.

If you've never been told by someone who just got hit by a car and is quite literally in one of the lowest points of their entire life that even *they* can't use your help and you're basically useless, let me tell you: it's not a great feeling. This moment, kneeling beside this man, feeling like an absolute useless bag of water, really just epitomized my general feeling about myself during this season of life. I was officially doubting my ridiculous decision to come here in the first place. Who on earth did I think I was and what was I doing here?

"Lizard Brain" refers to your limbic system, which is in charge of your flight, fight, and fear responses. I call my Lizard Brain my Gecko. And in this moment, my Gecko's whisper turned to a roar: "Go home. You don't belong here. You have nothing to offer."

The thing was, it was *true*. I really had no skills. No expertise. No job. No money. No plan. No vision. No real and useful knowledge or understanding of really anything.

Y'all.

That's a pretty demoralizing and pathetic place to be in life.

Until you realize . . .

Rock bottom is a *miraculous* place to channel your Inner Journalist. Perhaps in the last chapter The Scientists convinced you of the value of curiosity. But *how* do you start building your curiosity muscle? May I suggest that you engage in a little role play and pretend to be an award-winning investigative journalist on assignment in your very own life?

Here is the thing about journalists: the *good* ones start their quests for truth with as few ideas as possible about what they will uncover. A good, unbiased investigative journalist does not ask leading questions in an effort to simply confirm what they think they already know. They, in fact, assume they don't know the whole story and they ask questions out of a genuine sense of curiosity.

Then? (And this is the kicker!) They *actually listen* to the answer. They follow leads. And when an unexpected or new piece of information emerges? They abandon the well-trodden path they were on in favor of following the new lead into The Wilderness. And they do it all to get as close as possible to the honest-to-goodness truth. They do it because they know the very best stories are the truest ones and that the true ones usually have a few twists and turns along the way.

I decided that despite the fact that the *New York Times* never got back to me about that Dream Job (shocking, I know), I was going to, for all intents and purposes, act like the journalist I wanted to be. Because at least then, when people asked what I was doing with my life, I'd have an answer other than "Making a friend."

Yes! I would call myself a *journalist*. An *investigative journalist* at that.

Wait.

As long as I am essentially just making up a pretend role to play, let's go big: a (fun-employed) *foreign affairs investigative journalist* who goes by Elizabeth Ashley and has an English accent despite the fact that she grew up in the suburbs 30 miles from the Mississippi River.

NAILED IT.

So, I decided that from that moment on, employed to do so or not, I was simply going to channel my Inner Journalist. If I wanted to truly understand the issues facing women and girls living in extreme poverty and conflict and post-conflict zones, wasn't coming to the table a blank slate ready to ask questions and be surprised and follow leads the perfect place to start?

And herein lies the beauty of channeling your Inner Journalist: in that moment, my greatest insecurity (knowing nothing and having nothing to offer) became an *asset*. The less you think you have it all figured out, the more you can learn. The less you have riding on what you think you need to "discover," the freer you will be to get closer to the actual truth, whatever it may be. The more open you are to be surprised by what you uncover, the more likely you will be to find something *really* interesting.

So with a black-and-white composition notebook, I set out on a cross-country journey. I asked questions, listened to answers, and followed interesting leads to learn more and understand, straight from the source, the realities facing women and girls living in extreme poverty and/or post-conflict zones.

I initiated relationships. I invited people to coffee for informational meetings. I visited organizations and nonprofits and community-based projects to learn about what they were doing and why they were doing it that way. I hosted informal, small focus groups of young Ugandan women in borrowed living rooms where I served tea with *so much sugar*. (Just how Ugandans like it. My people.)

Through the friend I was living with at the time, I was introduced to an organization with the mission of finding and equipping the brightest youth in East Africa to become leaders in their communities and our world. That friend introduced me to another friend, I followed some leads, and before I knew it, I hopped onto a dairy truck that transported milk between a rural ranch and the city. About halfway through the dusty journey, I jumped off and landed in a magical corner of the universe in the form of a girl's leadership academy. There I met the most incredible group of young women that I've ever had the privilege of knowing.

I may have set out to meet just one girl, but lucky me, there were about 25 of them. After spending time out at the school, the leaders eventually asked me to help contribute to their quarterly donor newsletter, which gave me the perfect school-sanctioned excuse to use that fancy journalism degree and call students out of the lunch room to sit on the lawn under the mango tree and ask them questions.* It gave me the chance to learn, not from a World Bank or Gates Foundation report, but *straight from the source*, the experience of being born a female in Uganda. Their challenges, their joys, their fears, and their audacious hopes about the future.

These young women came from every corner of Uganda. Many came from backgrounds of extreme poverty. Some had lost either one or both of their parents. And far too many of these precious, complex, brilliant, resilient girls had experienced some form of trauma, sexual violence, or loss that would break your heart right open.

I met women like Muteteli, a Rwandan immigrant whose family lived the horrors of genocide and was in the messy and excruciating and worthy process of trying to rebuild and heal.

Like Joan, who as a young girl held her mother's hand as she died from a preventable respiratory disease and then assumed the responsibility for her eight siblings.

Like Betty, who lost both of her parents in childhood. With no one to support her, she would go early and stay late after school and clean the grounds to help pay off her school fees. When she finally made it to high school, she couldn't find a job in the entire country of Uganda, so she moved to South Sudan

---

*By the way, I learned from the leadership at this remarkable organization to never, ever, ever publish or share information without explicit consent from those who shared it. You would never in a million years share sensitive information about a co-worker or your friend's child on your Instagram page without their permission. Why on God's Green Earth would we think about sharing the story of a 17-year-old Ugandan without permission and informed consent? Doesn't matter if it's for a "good cause." The ends do not justify the means.

by herself to work for two years as nursery school teacher, until she had enough money saved up to come back to Uganda and pay her school fees.

Like Beatrice, who grew up in the height of the conflict in Northern Uganda. Every night she and her brothers would walk with other kids to the center of town where they would get locked in a machine shop that the adults would guard overnight in an attempt to keep the children from being kidnapped by the Lord's Resistance Army. In spite of this, over the course of the next year, every single one of her brothers was captured.

And yet, despite the unimaginable obstacles the women faced, they were some of the brightest lights I've ever met. Not only were they academically gifted (top 5 percent of students in the country), their vision for their futures and how they would impact their families, communities, country, and ultimately our world was *astounding* to me. I'd listen to their stories of trauma and heartache and think, *Lord have mercy.* If that had been me, I'd be in a dark closet in the fetal position, and yet, here *they* were continuing to dream these bold and beautiful dreams and actually taking the steps toward making them happen by defying all odds and pursuing their high school degrees from one of the best, most competitive schools in the country.

Globally, more than 130 million girls are denied access to education.[1] The average woman in Uganda has about five years of schooling.[2] Yet we know that every single extra year of school a woman receives reduces the mortality rate for children. Globally, educating women accounts for 51 percent of the decline in mortality—the biggest influence *by far*.[3]

An educated woman is less likely to be a victim of domestic abuse and less likely to be married as a child. If and when she chooses to become a mother, she is more likely to have healthier children who receive more education. Uganda is not unique in that if women are precluded from education and therefore positions of influence and power, the systemic issues facing women and girls in all income brackets will likely not progress.

For example, in Uganda, women do not have equal protection from the law in regard to property ownership and inheritance,[4] which has devastating implications for the most vulnerable members of society. Over 50 percent of Ugandans believe that a husband is justified in hitting or beating his wife, and a similar percentage of women have experienced intimate partner violence.[5] Despite attempts over the past 50 years to amend the Marriage and Divorce Bill, to this day, marital rape is not considered a crime.*

And I'm telling you point-blank that an idealistic, naive, white 22-year-old American isn't going to change any of that.

But you know who is? *These* young women. As they meandered across their beautifully lush high school campus in their matching plaid skirts and navy sweaters, I listened in on heated debates about the implications of the bride price tradition and land rights and the cultural taboo surrounding sexual violence. I sat under the mango tree, witnessing magic, as they dared to dream about being in the 2 percent of women in their country who would continue on to university and become the lawyers and the politicians and the university professors and the social workers who would change the game for themselves and the girls who come after them. I

---

*And if you're American, before you get too high on your horse, remember that the rates of intimate partner violence in our country are still around 30 percent. We did not legally criminalize marital rape until 1993.

knew, in the deepest part of my soul, that ultimately *they* were the solution.

But as I continued to lean into this new community, asking questions and *listening*, I learned about a very specific and consistent concern many of these young women shared: in just a few months, they would graduate from this two-year college-prep high school. They would enter into their "gap," which is a nine-month period between high school and college when most of them would return home and try to find a job and save money to pay for university tuition.

And these young women were unanimously concerned.

Not just about the money. Although with an incredibly high youth unemployment rate and young women being 50 percent more likely to be unemployed, being able to find a job—any job—was certainly a concern.[6]

But they were also concerned about what would happen when they went back home during this break. They were concerned about returning home and the potential lack of support to continue their education, mainly in the form of the pressure to get married and have children instead.

And when I say *pressure*, you must understand that I'm not talking about a passive-aggressive remark or side-eye from your mom every now and then. Some of these young women would return to families living in extreme poverty and may be seen as one of the few hopes of an income through their "bride price," which is the payment their families will receive for their hands in marriage.

She might face the choice to "save" her family, whom she loves deeply and sacrificially, by agreeing to marry a 40-year-old man—and while her bride price of a cow and two goats may temporarily relieve a short-term financial burden, it doesn't begin to chip away at extreme generational poverty. Of course, she won't have met this man, and most likely he won't consider his new 19-year-old bride his equal. She might enter into a marriage where she cannot even co-own property with her husband, which means if he dies, his extended family may have the legal right to come and claim every bit of the life they built together: her home, her land, and any financial assets they've accrued together. By marrying him, she'll forfeit the right to claim domestic abuse or even rape because, don't be silly, it's impossible to "abuse" and "rape" your own marital property.

So, yeah. She's a wee bit concerned about the upcoming "summer break."

And before I knew it, so was I. Because that's what happens when you channel your Inner Journalist and go to the primary source, instead of just relying on other people's reports. The information and the facts and the figures weave their way into stories so complex and heartbreaking and brilliantly bright that you can no longer not be concerned.

By channeling my Inner Journalist, I went from aimless and overwhelmed by Global Extreme Poverty and Gender Inequality and All The Big Problems to listening, learning, and leaning in.

I had found my beat.

One community.

25 women.

A nine-month gap.

No billions of people. No million-dollar budgets. No fancy policy efforts. No global initiatives just

One community.

25 women.

Nine months.

I hope you believe by now that it's okay to start out by trading in those big, impressive dreams for tiny, beautiful ones. But if you're wondering *how* those tiny, beautiful dreams emerge in the first place, this is it.

It doesn't matter if you're truly just starting out or if you're decades in. Either way: be on assignment in your own life.

Show up like a cub reporter, new on the beat. Start looking around and ask interesting questions, not needing to confirm your preexisting biases. You don't need to prove to everyone around you that you've got it all figured out. In fact, it's infinitely easier to learn when you know you don't. Show up with a pure, truth-seeking, nothing-to-lose sense of curiosity and I all but guarantee a Tiny Dream will emerge.

And if at first, this makes you feel a little uncomfortable because your entire life you've been taught to act like you know it all, feel free to start out by channeling your inner, insatiably curious journalist until it becomes an extension of who are you and how you operate in the world.

Stay awake. Ask the questions, look for the clues, follow the leads wherever they may take you.

SIX

Find and Replace

When I was in fourth grade, we got our first family desktop computer. It was a Gateway computer and it came in a giant cow-print box and we all crammed into the "home office" while my dad opened the box and showcased our shiny, new technology toy.

A few weeks into using it, while working on a school paper, I noticed an odd thing: every time I typed my name (which you have to do for *every* school paper) it auto-changed my name into a series of frowning faces.

Just a few weeks prior to this, I had rebelled, snuck out of bed, and watched an R-rated Stephen King movie on *TNT* called *Maximum Overdrive*, where various mechanical objects are possessed, come to life, and wreak havoc on their human owners in an over-the-top gory and traumatizing manner. (It stars Emilio Estevez and currently has a Rotten Tomatoes approval rating of 12 percent if you're interested in a nice Friday-night flick with your honey.)

I was an impressionable young thing, and so when the family computer started replacing my name with frowning faces, I *obviously* assumed that the beloved 100-pound computer was turning on us and had begun torturing me with subtle hints that I would be its first gruesome victim. I couldn't tell my parents without incriminating myself and pleading guilty to staying up past my bedtime and watching an R-rated movie, so for weeks, I suffered in silent terror as every time I typed my name, it automatically turned it into the frowny faces that were a sign of my impending death.

Turns out, my brother Pat, who was in fifth grade at the time and would have been considered a bit of a tech genius by mid-'90s standards, was responsible for cleverly enabling a "Find and Replace" action that "found" my name and "replaced" it with a row of frowning faces. Very cute, big brother. Very cute.

Although the remnants of the psychological damage caused by the ordeal still remain today, I learned an important concept for which I am eternally grateful: *Find and Replace.*

It's not just a Microsoft Word trick. You can use this as a life/mind hack on your journey to building a life of purpose, passion, and impact.

Most of us have been taught to go out and find the shiny, sexy, innovative *solution.* In fact, our entire education system is oriented toward being handed a problem and then trying to find the solution.

And the "problem" so many people are faced with today is the question being handed to them: What is your passion and purpose? Why are you here? And people are running around like crazed, passion-eating zombies looking for The Solution without even really having identified the problem.

Compose the hit song.

Build the hot app.

Write the buzzy book.

Get married to the soul mate.

Start the charity.

Get the right degree from the right college.

Launch the company.

Build the social media platform.

Score the dream job.

Solutions, solutions, solutions.

But let's flip this on its head: What if becoming really, really good at *finding* problems *before* jumping to the supposed solution is actually the best place to start?

What if every time we thought we should be looking for *THE* solution, we **Found and Replaced** "Solution" with what design theorist Horst Rittel calls a "Wicked Problem?"[1] (Or what I call a Really Juicy Problem.)

Now, some of you might be thinking to yourself, *Lady, stahhhp. What do you mean go* find *problems? I've got more problems than I know what to do with and you're telling me to go look for more? This book is a crock. I want a refund!*

Simmer down and hear me out.

Interesting problems will actually *solve* some of your more uninteresting problems, because you will slowly *lose your ability* to care about things that don't really matter.

Now, listen, there are certainly problems that won't disappear: sick kids and ageing parents and failing health. But I promise once you get good at finding Really Juicy Problems, you will start to lose interest in and awareness of all the problems you once thought were worth your time.

What will they think of me?
What if I don't say the right thing?
What if I look stupid? Or worse, *ambitious*?
What if they knew how much we fought?
What if they knew how much money I really make?
What if I look like a bad mom?
What if they see me in yesterday's clothes?
What if they talk about me behind my back?

How do I get a flatter stomach?
How can I be a part of the "in" crowd?
How do I come across as put together?
How do I prove I'm good enough?
How do I keep up?
    with the car I drive
    and the clothes I wear
    and where my kids get into college
    and how fast I get promoted
    and the Pinterest-worthy house?!

Once you decide to give the (very limited) plucks you have to a few Really Juicy Problems, you just don't have leftover steam for all the uninteresting ones.

When you finally figure out what *your* Really Juicy Problems are, every time a new problem comes your way you will ask yourself: Does solving *this* small problem get me one step closer to solving the Really Juicy Problems? And if the answer is "no" that problem will slowly start to lose its power over you. Your energy and time and brain power are so precious and you just don't have time for stupid problems, Pluckie.

Basically, Really Juicy Problems are Stupid Problem *annihilators*.

* * *

Not only will being a purveyor of Really Juicy Problems help you get rid of your stupid, small problems, it's integral to living a life of purpose and impact. While the world may be obsessed with The Solutions, we know that being able to find, identify, and stay committed to Interesting Problems is much more valuable. Charles Kettering said, "A problem well-stated is a problem half solved."[2] Instead of jumping to the solutions, let's get better at finding and stating *real* and juicy problems.

For everyone, but *especially* for my generation who grew up being told they could "Change the World!"* a very precarious thing can happen when we get so enamored with bright and shiny "solutions" instead of staying focused on actually solving interesting problems. We become so obsessed with the solution and we pour our energy into chasing it without much regard to whether the Solution *is actually solving the problem*. We start with and get emotionally attached to The Solution, when we should be having a committed love affair with The Interesting Problem.

---

*A general rule of thumb for us "World Changers" is that the further you are from the problem and the less you are *personally* affected by it, the more you should assume a posture of curiosity and learning and openness. The more you should first focus on being someone who is really good at *finding and understanding* interesting problems before immediately jumping to the sexy, shiny solution.

If you're reading this book, I am going to assume you are someone who hopes that the work and the forward movement of your life might not only help you unlock your truest self but might also create a little bit of light and freedom and opportunity for others.*

Being "solutions agnostic" is a fantastic mindset for anyone, but *especially* if you're someone who wants to make a positive impact in the world. We mustn't get so obsessed with our solutions that we stop asking, nearly constantly, "Am I *actually* helping to solve the Interesting Problem?"

It's not a one-time thing. It's a forever and ever mentality I'm asking you to adopt. It's a terrifying and humbling and vulnerable and *incredibly necessary* part of the journey.

The good news is, especially for those of you feeling frustrated or demoralized because you haven't "found your passion" or "settled on a solution," that you can stop beating yourself up and instead start congratulating yourself! If you don't already have a death grip on The Solution it's infinitely easier to ask these important and juicy questions. This is your Beginner's edge!

✻ ✻ ✻

I had no idea of what I had to offer by way of a solution, but by asking questions and following leads, I had discovered a Really Juicy Problem: *25 of the brightest, academically qualified women in Uganda might not go to university because they lacked the financial and social support to do so.*

It was the ***problem*** (figuring some way to help bright young women go to college so they could go on to become leaders

---

*Hint: if your purpose doesn't in some capacity overflow goodness and light to those around you, it's not your true purpose. It's a Red Herring. And it will likely eventually turn you into a jerk. Buyer beware!

in their communities) not the specific **solution** that became my obsessive and passionate focus.

Find and Replace.

Now that I had found my Really Juicy Problem that was interesting enough to keep me awake at night, it was time to start thinking about potential solutions.

Just how would we bridge the nine-month gap between high school and college these young women were heading into?

Now, here is where I get to be brutally honest with you: there were a few key words in this particular Really Juicy Problem that triggered a set of beliefs I brought along with me (in my ridiculous mountaineering backpack that also held my powdered outer-space food) when I showed up in Uganda. These key words? Africa, poverty, marginalized women.

Given the single narrative I had come to believe about Africa, *THE* solution felt pretty immediately clear to me. Start some kind of philanthropy. Duh. Launch a nonprofit that would mobilize the resources to *give* money to bridge the gap between high school and university so that these young women could go on to become change makers in their community.

DONE.

NAILED IT.

ONWARD!

Within virtually no time, not only had I decided to start a charity but I had a pretty clear vision for exactly how this solution would work. It would be sponsorship based. We'd match up a woman in the U.S. with one woman in Uganda, largely based on their education and career interests. These American women would sponsor their Ugandan counterparts. They'd do some fundraising, cut them a check, and wham bam.

Girl goes to college.

Girl changes the world.

My work here is done!

You know how much confidence I felt that I could pull this off?

Pretty confident, actually.*

I had a communications background. I could whip up a logo, mission, and impact messaging, no problem. I had volunteered or interned for at least half a dozen nonprofits during my time in college and felt pretty familiar with the fundraising, advocacy, grant-writing world.

It seemed like I had just arrived in the little corner of the universe where my skill set and experience could be put to use to solve a problem I cared about. Which meant gotcha!! *I had finally found* My Passion and managed to snag it by its rascally tail. It was time to get work! (Work that would never *feel* like work, because after all, I HAD FOUND MY PASSION!)

❖ ❖ ❖

Luckily, although I had this *solution* in mind (starting a sponsorship-based philanthropy to send young women to college) I was still channeling my Inner Journalist. I had spent the last few months traveling the country, trying to learn as much as possible about The Problem. Even though I did think this charity idea was a no-brainer solution, before I started anything, I was going to apply that same investigative journalist scrutiny and curiosity to the solutions side of the equation.

Who was already doing something like this? How were they structured? What were the outcomes? I knew this was not a

*GASP, I know. Us women are never supposed to so readily admit our confidence in our abilities! Burn this book!

ground-breaking idea. I was going to apply a fairly simple, charitable sponsorship model to a very specific community problem. Not rocket science, people. No need to reinvent the wheel.

So off I went, composition notebook in hand, to learn as much as possible. Curious to understand the good, the bad, and the ugly.

I'll keep this somewhat brief, as the content of the next paragraph could be a whole book on its own. But as I started to delve deeper into the world of Ugandan nonprofits, sponsorship projects, and international charities, the water got murkier than my Bless Your Heart Idealistic Self had anticipated. And the moment I started sensing that all was not quite as I had imagined, it sent me into full-on *Frontline–60 Minutes–20/20–Dateline* mode.

But instead of crumbling into a state of jaded cynicism, my curiosity was triggered, and I slipped back into my investigative journalist mentality.

I wanted to really understand. I wanted to ask difficult questions and follow interesting leads.

So I did. I sought out the smartest Ugandans I could find who I could convince to give me the time of day. I asked them the hard questions and I tried to really listen and understand their answers. I pitched them on the best idea *I* had for a solution. *Of course* I wanted to hear, "Yes! Your charity idea is a brilliant solution to the problem, Liz!" because let me be very clear: I have an Ego that loves noshing affirmation.

But *the only reason* I could genuinely ask for honest feedback on my idea is because I had *no specific solution* to protect. I only had a fledgling, weeks old, half-baked idea, to which I had zero emotional attachment.

When a *good* journalist discovers that their theory might be off, they don't get defensive. They say, *Tell me more.* They follow leads. So I picked my notebook back up and went down a long and twisty path, traveling around the country asking increasingly difficult questions about sustainability and foreign aid and the unintended consequences of the NGO sector in Uganda.

And with each day that passed, and with each bit of feedback from people I trusted that I received, I became more and more uneasy about my little charity idea. I started to see more and more flaws in my plan. I started to wonder if this was actually the best solution I could muster.

Was it a bit unsettling? Sure. No one likes to admit their idea isn't great.

Were there times I was tempted to just stop asking questions and do the thing that felt pretty within my capabilities and comfort zone to do? *Absolutely.*

But the truth of the matter is, I wasn't committed to the solution. I was committed to The Really Juicy Problem.

Find and replace.

And while I believe there are phenomenal nonprofits doing *remarkable* work, the more digging I did, the more I realized that I couldn't ignore the fact that when I started really trying to understand how nations and regions develop, it had a lot to do with economic growth, job creation, and trade policy.

And perhaps most earth-shatteringly, I started to become increasingly uncomfortable with how many foreign charities have contributed to a social and relational dynamic between Westerners and Africans that made me incredibly uncomfortable. This notion that somehow, simply by being White and

Western I was there to play the role of "Giver" and Africans were to assume the role of "Grateful Beneficiary."

I believe that we are called to live in community with others, across the street and across the globe. Community where we do this sacred dance together through seasons of needing and being needed. Giving and receiving. Barely staying above water one minute and being the lifesaver the next. It's how humans are designed to exist together, pushing us all toward greater empathy and dignity and unity. In *any relationship*, when we start to get confused and think these seasons and circumstances are permanent roles we are meant to play, we strip ourselves and others of the dignity of being a dynamic, complex, fellow human who is both terribly broken and brilliantly bright.

The more questions I asked and the more I surrounded myself with people who were smarter than me, the more I started questioning everything I thought I knew about how to "Change the World."

Instead, *my* whole world started to turn upside down.

One day while drinking tea with Nnyabo Monica, who was the headmistress of the girl's school, she looked at me and said, "Liz. Instead of giving the girls money, why don't you do something so that the girls can *earn* their money? Something where they can *learn skills* and where they *can stay together.*"

As I listened to her explain all the reasons she thought this would be a better approach than my charity idea, I heard her say things like "earn money" and "learn skills" and I started to get the sneaking suspicion that perhaps business could be the tool to help solve The Interesting Problem.

Wait. *What?* NO. (More on why this was *shocking* to me in the next chapter.)

I didn't know it at the time, but had I shown up in Uganda with some airtight plan or agenda or know-it-all posture, I am 100 percent sure that this beautiful, messy, heartbreaking, and joy-giving business I've spent the last ten years cultivating and building wouldn't exist. Because it's *really difficult* to truly ask interesting questions if you think you've already got it all figured out.

Confirmation bias is "the tendency to interpret new evidence as confirmation of one's existing beliefs or theories."[3] And I think it's one of the strongest and most innate desires we have as humans. Our beliefs are so very core to who we are and where we belong that to do anything that could threaten them is *scary*.

Which means it is *really hard* to ask honest questions and really listen to the answers when there is a possibility that those answers might contradict your existing beliefs or theories.

I'm truly convinced that the only reason I didn't suffer this common fate isn't because I was super self-aware or morally superior. The less flattering, more honest truth is that I wasn't bullheaded about my solution because *I didn't have a specific solution in mind.* I didn't have a vision. I was a little bit aimless. I hadn't yet found my thing, my solution, or my Dream Job. And not for a lack of trying.

I had managed to find a Really Juicy Problem but I was "solutions agnostic."

And only by being more obsessively focused on the problem than I was on implementing a certain solution did I become, begrudgingly, convinced by Headmistress Monica and others, that *this specific interesting problem* didn't need to be solved by a charity, but with a sustainable marketplace solution.

※　※　※

After realizing I needed to start *a business*, I was at an utter and complete loss.

Zero ideas. Nada. Zilch. Nothing.

Struggle bus, you guys.

As I sat staring down that blank wall at a complete and utter loss for what exactly this business could be, I did what anyone who has taken a Business 101 class (which I had not) would have done.

Market Research!

HA. LYING.

More like I walked outside and saw a guy that had about 106 live chickens tied to the back of his motorcycle. Once the sheer awe of this sight wore off, I felt like I started to see chickens everywhere. Chickens on the back of his motorcycle. Chickens in the market. Chickens running across a living room. Seemed like people were into the chicken thing here.

Guess I'll start a chicken farm!

That half-baked (or shall we say over-easy? Ba-da-ching!) idea didn't last very long.

In those few weeks a couple of things became very clear: the math didn't add up. I wanted each woman to be able to earn an income that could contribute significantly to her future college tuition and for reasons I won't get into here, a boot-strapped chicken farm in the time frame I was working with wasn't going to cut it.

So, I gave up the chicken ghost and put to rest yet another crappy idea.

RIP, chicken farm!

However demoralizing, with each "failed" solution I established a few more parameters that would get me one step closer to a better solution.

So after chicken farmer, I moved to shoe designer.

I'd share with you exactly how I got from one to the other, but isn't it kind of obvious?

Ha. Kidding. I'll tell you that later, but first I'll leave you with this: do not be fooled by the notion that in order to build a life of purpose and impact you must be the Keeper and Defender of your precious ideas and solutions. That is not your job. Your first and most important job is to be the seeker and finder of interesting problems.

Find and replace solutions with problems.

If your problem is more important than your solution, you will be free to ask the questions you're most afraid to ask. And when you must let a solution go? Do not despair. This process of having to let go and reimagining is not a stumbling block or an obstacle keeping you from the work. This is the *very work* that you were created to do.

SEVEN

Surprise Yourself

My sophomore year of college I made the trek down Highway 70 from Columbia, Missouri, to St. Louis for Thanksgiving. After greeting my dad, who has a background in accounting and finance, I announced to him that after much consideration, I intended to tack on a Gender Studies minor to my journalism degree. He was like, "*Really*? We don't think one liberal arts degree is enough? Maybe you could go for something a wee bit more marketable like a business minor? Just a *minor*, that's all I ask!"

The *audacity*.

In hindsight, that sure seems like a reasonable, dare I say wise suggestion, but in the moment, in the way only a 20-year-old who has the world entirely figured out can, I responded to him as if he had just suggested I sell my vital organs on a black market intended to help keep war criminals alive. It was all the proof I needed that clearly my father didn't know me, if he thought I'd step foot in a *business* class.

After all, I was an idealistic, principled journalism student who cared about social justice and Other Very Important Things. I believed that if you were passionate about business, there was a good chance your main interest in life was helping the rich get richer and building your own little kingdom of wealth, regardless of the cost to anyone else.

Business was a part of the problem. So, in response to my father's suggestion: No. Case closed. Thank you, next.

Now, I can't remember exactly what I was wearing during that conversation, but I have a pretty good guess because my uniform in college consisted mainly of thrifted "genie" pants,* a kelly-green puffer vest, and a John Deere hat I found abandoned on the sidewalk of my college campus. I was a "freegan" who prayed for my friends who were super into fashion because I basically knew before they even opened their precious mouths that if they cared about fashion it went without saying that they were pretty shallow, materialistic, and definitely had no idea where Syria was. Thanks, but no thanks. I'll be over here saving the world with the words no one will pay me to write while you're browsing Nordstrom.com and RUINING EVERYTHING.

Business? Ew.

Fashion? Woof.

Sweet baby Jesus. Bless me and my judgmental, self-righteous 20-year-old heart. If you ever need a firsthand account of just how Humble Pie tastes, this part of my story is basically a detailed foodie review of that rich and complex flavor profile. Nom, nom, nom.

---

*My sweet college roommates had to stage an intervention to get me out of the infamous genie pants I had purchased at a secondhand market in Uganda and into real clothes for what ended up being my surprise engagement. My level of commitment to terrible style was almost admirable.

It took several years, but the crunchy, genie-pant-wearing, anti–The Man capitalism-hater is now the CEO of a for-profit, real-life, tax-paying, employee-employing *fashion* company.

AND I LOVE IT.

I can say unequivocally that, today, one of my deepest passions is using *business* to solve the problems that are typically left to the nonprofit sector to figure out. When I hear about a Big Hairy Audacious Problem currently being solved with a traditional charity or nonprofit model, I immediately start thinking about if perhaps there is a more scalable, mutually beneficial marketplace solution for that very same problem.

I'm also wildly passionate about creating beautifully designed, versatile, ethically manufactured products. It's not just a day job for me. I think about these things while I am in the shower. I dream about them. I can't get enough of helping women discover their style and build a wardrobe full of beautiful products with beautiful stories behind them.

It's obsessive.

It's compulsive.

It's passion.

Business and fashion.

Could *not* have seen that coming. But what I've learned in the decade since is that when you channel your Inner Beginner, you let yourself be surprised by what might make you come alive.

While your **why** will always be most important, make no mistake, the **what** does matter. If you're not energized at all by the actual day-to-day work, you won't make it. As sold-out and passionate and obsessed as I was with the **why** (employing academically gifted young women and creating a launch pad for them to pursue their dreams and become leaders in their communities) it wouldn't be enough to keep me going to build something truly meaningful unless the **what** (the tasks and activities that will fill the hours that will make up our days and eventually our lives) is also aligned with who I am created to be.

But! You must be willing to be surprised to find interest and passion and intrigue where you least expect it.

* * *

As I mentioned earlier, a few weeks into the Chicken Farmer gig it became clear it didn't make sense from a business perspective. But what I didn't tell you is that it also became *abundantly clear* that I was not the woman for the chicken farming job. Literally *nothing* about chickens or the idea of running a chicken farm, even for the best of causes, made me feel anything other than sheer dread and a little bit of disgust, to be honest.

Those beady little black chicken eyes? That unsettling head and neck movement that feels kind of aggressive and strangely intimidating? AND THOSE FEET? Those decrepit claws that look like a disgruntled, decaying, three-fingered grandma with an ax to grind is reaching out from her shallow grave at midnight to make her first move of revenge?

It all sparked zero curiosity or light within me. It didn't make my heart beat even a little bit faster. (Except out of fear of having an eye gouged out by a rogue chicken beak.) A few weeks into working on this idea, there was no delight, joy, or intrigue.

Just nada.

I was dead inside.

And I gave up my chicken farming aspirations.*

* * *

A lot of people will pursue a **what** that they enjoy or are decent at without ever doing the hard work of figuring out their **why**. It might work for some time, but after a while, a sneaking suspicion emerges that they were *made for more*. They are unable to tap into the gold mine of intrinsic motivation because they don't know their **why**. They long for a sense of purpose and to be a part of a story that is bigger than "I do something I'm decent at and I make enough money doing it."

Then there are others who understand the importance of the **why**. They deeply desire to have meaning and purpose in their work and life. But they mistakenly believe that if the **why** is good and true enough, the **how** and the **what** doesn't matter. In an effort to create an impact, there can be a level of self-denial and a sort of martyrdom. People are surprised when, although the work they are doing is important and meaningful, the actual mechanics of their work doesn't interest or ignite them and they eventually start to feel drained, frustrated, and burned out.

Understanding the things that bring you to life and make you tick *are* important.

---

*I currently live in Portland, Oregon, on an urban commune. With chickens. Because, if you're going to live in Portland, just go big on the Portlandia stereotypes, you know? It's like these chickens that I am supposed to feel affection for are just daily reminders of my chicken-farming failure. Each morning when I open my windows I hear nothing but: bock-bock-baFAILURE. That being said, I realize this confession about my chicken fear and disgust will likely land me on Portland's version of a terrorist watch list. What respectable Portland hipster doesn't love chickens?

BUT that being said, if you want to build a life of passion and purpose, you're best off if you're willing to be surprised by what it looks like. You might actually build a passionate life doing something that *in a million years*, you'd never have been able to see coming. And you will never know unless you are open enough to try. You'll never be surprised if you're running every idea through a 12-point checklist and making sure it aligns perfectly with everything you *think* you know about your interests and gifts and experience and natural inclinations.

If you're open to explore, you're probably a little more likely to bomb a few times in the short term. But I truly believe that if you expect to be surprised by your purpose and passion, you're also infinitely more likely to succeed *in the long run.* When you stay open to the possibility of surprising yourself, you stop hanging out on the sidelines, looking for the thing that makes perfect sense, *before* you finally hop in the game.

I was not the kid who grew up executing darling entrepreneurial ventures or doing fashion sketches or playing dress up in my mom's closet. There were just no signs that I'd go on to run a fashion company. No "I've always been passionate about . . ." No "Ever since I was a little kid . . ." tales to tell that would support the notion that my passion was inside me the whole time. That's *Find Your Passion* propaganda, you guys!

OK, OK. Maybe that experience *is* true for some people. But that's not how it happens for a lot of us. And to believe in this single narrative contributes to keeping us more focused on "finding" a passion that "makes sense." And what I want you to have is the freedom to be insatiably curious *problem finders* who expect to be surprised (and delighted!) by what you discover about yourself in the process.

* * *

After the chicken farm failed, a mentor in Uganda who was much wiser than I and who had a very vested interest in seeing these young women continue on to university suggested I pursue something I was a little more familiar with than Ugandan chickens. "You're an American woman. Surely you know what they like? Why not make something *you'd* want to buy and then go home and sell it?"

OK. Point taken. I *am* slightly more familiar with American women than Ugandan chickens.

Think of something American women would buy . . .

But *WHAT*?

While Skype-ing with an old college roommate and telling her about my conundrum, she casually mentioned the strappy, funky sandals that I made back when we were in school. Toward the end of my college career, while I was walking across campus one day, I was so annoyed by the sound of my flip flops. I thought to myself, *Self, wouldn't it be nice if you had a pair of flip flops that didn't flop?**

So after class, I went back to my house and sat on the front porch and took that pair of cheap, rubber flip flops and tore off the plastic thong piece and replaced it with some funky, rainbow-striped ribbon. And voila! Flip flops that didn't flop!

NAILED IT.

And you know what was funny to me at the time? People noticed these strappy, funky sandals. *And thought they were cute*. HA! As if that was the point! In fact, a few people even

---

*I know it's probably shocking to you that given this caliber of intellectual quandary, I was walking to an entry-level geology class and not a graduate level PhD philosophy class.

asked me to make them a pair. "I'll pay you for them," they said! But because I had more important things to do, like saving the world with my words, I told them no. (Comical, considering that now my entire life basically consists of trying to convince people to BUY *MY* SANDALS PLEASE.*)

When my friend from back home referenced those strappy, homemade sandals, I ran it through my short list of newly established parameters and upon first glance, it seemed to check at least a few boxes.

Was I *passionate* about those sandals and the idea of making footwear or anything that would fall into the general "fashion" category?

Not really.

Was I *thrilled* by the prospect of running a best-in-class vertically integrated manufacturing company in East Africa?

Nope, not in the least.

Exactly zero childhood dreams or desires fulfilled.

But was I *as* disgusted by this prospect as I was by chickens?

Also, no!

WINNING!

(Alternative title of this book: *10 Steps to Lowering Your Standards: A Guide to Finding Your Passion. And Having a Happier Marriage*. Kidding!)†

Had I "found" my passion? It certainly didn't feel like it. But these sandals did feel like a possible solution to *The REALLY JUICY PROBLEM* that didn't make me want to gag or cry. So I kept going. A little further and a little deeper. One foot in front of the other, step by step, making the path by walking it. And boy did that path surprise me.

*www.ssekodesigns.com.
†Mostly.

With *zero* preexisting interest in fashion, I just never could have predicted it. But the designing and the prototyping and the satisfaction that came from seeing something that once only existed in my mind become an object I could hold in my hands?

It absolutely lit my soul on fire.

I'd stay up until 3 AM with fingers bloody from rogue scissor slashes that occurred while attempting to cut through thick leather hides, bleary-eyed but entirely unable to stop tinkering with these strappy sandals.

I'd fall asleep for a few hours surrounded by a pile of leather scraps and then wake up the next morning and spend the day tracking down suppliers and costing out materials and researching and negotiating and figuring out how all the pieces fit together to build a real-life *business*. I'd walk out of a three-hour long meeting with the hard-bargaining Ugandan guy who imported rubber from Kenya and realize that my face was hurting from smiling at the sheer (and surprising) thrill of it all.

❊ ❊ ❊

Fast-forward a few years. I was now operating a scrappy little sandal company with about a dozen employees out of a house right next to Mackerere University in a bustling part of Kampala. The living room had been converted into the sewing headquarters while under the covered porch and the mango trees that dotted the property, women were cutting leather and assembling sandal soles.

One day I had a friend of a friend reach out about an exceptional young woman around my age who was looking for work. The only problem was, nearly every day I was being approached by someone who needed a job. But we were still a tiny, threadbare company and were not regularly hiring. On the rare occasion that we did, we'd tell our existing team that we had a new position open and by daybreak on Monday morning there would be a line of women at our compound gate, eager for the chance to interview.

I told this acquaintance that we were, unfortunately, not hiring and had no plans to in the immediate future. I could barely pay the employees I had and definitely not myself. But he insisted that I meet her—a "kindred spirit," supposedly—and so I agreed.

Agnes and I met at our house-gone-sandal-factory. I closed the door to a bedroom we had converted into an office, and there we sat, sipping sugary black tea from bright, primary-colored plastic mugs.

Sure enough, we hit it off. She shared with me about her experience growing up and how her father (who was raising her and her sister on his own) was offered an enormous bride price from an elder in their village for her hand in marriage when she was only fifteen. To the shock and surprise of the entire village, he declined the offer in favor of keeping his daughter in school,* where she continued to excel through high school and eventually university. Throughout school, she was at the top of her class and started forming a Big Dream about working for the United Nations. She had learned at an early age the enormous challenges young women and children in Uganda face and she wanted to be a part of creating change in a BIG WAY.

She graduated with honors from university and started the job hunt, and to her horror, experienced firsthand just how

*#DadGoals!

difficult this path would be. Despite her impressive diploma and glowing recommendations, at *every single job interview* she attended, with varying degrees of explicitness, she was propositioned for sex by the male interviewer. She left each experience feeling more demoralized and demeaned than the last. If this was the challenge that *she* was facing, she couldn't imagine what it would be like for her sisters who were less educated and confident and privileged. As her frustration grew, so did her commitment to creating dignified opportunity for women in her community.

As we continued to chat, we were interrupted no less than six times. I'd hear a knock on the office door and reply, "Come in." Each time it was someone in need of a supply.

We've run out of leather. Have we ordered more?

There is no more white thread, only black. Should we substitute?

The scissors have become too dull and need sharpening. Shall I run into town?

After the door closed yet again and we resumed our conversation, Agnes spoke up in a kind but matter-of-fact way. She suggested that perhaps we could use some help with the systems we were using to keep our supplies, tools, and raw materials in stock. "Of course," I said, too exasperated and in agreement to be defensive of our *painfully* inefficient production process. "But we just can't afford to hire someone to do that right now. To be honest, we're barely making ends meet." Where I saw a mundane and frustrating part of our chaotic startup, Agnes saw an opportunity.

"Let me do it." she replied.

"Excuse me?"

"Give me *one month* to help organize your processes and supplies. I'll be an intern. You don't even have to pay me. After one month, you'll see that the money I can save you in time alone could justify a full-time position. Just one month. You'll see."

Now, if I've got a weak spot, an Achilles' heel, it's precisely *that* kind of pluck.

It was an offer I couldn't refuse.

"Well, okay then, Agnes."

"Wonderful. You can call me Aggie."

Within a few weeks, she had been officially hired. Within a year, she completely transformed our production systems. Within a few more, she was leaving Uganda for the first time to head to Nairobi, Kenya, to meet with our largest raw materials suppliers and negotiate pricing, terms, and quality standards. As our Director of Procurement, she joined the senior-level management team who ran everything from our supply chain and production to accounting and human resources.

One hot Thursday afternoon, a man in a crisply pressed suit walked into our workshop during the lunch hour and approached the table where the managers were seated, finishing their meal. He explained that he was from the state house and that the president wished to meet with the director of Sseko Designs. While everyone fell silent in understandable disbelief that the president of Uganda was summoning us, Aggie—by far the youngest manager, but the first to stand up—simply said, "Well, let's go, then!" Hours later she found herself in the office of the president. Earlier that year, his wife, Janet, had been gifted a pair of Sseko Sandals. When Janet shared with her husband that her new sandals were made in Uganda, he was in disbelief and requested to meet with the leadership of this company.

When Aggie (she was in her midtwenties at the time) walked into his office, he took one look at her and said to the aide who escorted her in, "Why did you bring me a 16-year-old girl when I requested to meet with the director?"

Aggie responded confidently, "That's me, sir. And I am here to tell you about the best manufacturing company in our country. What do you want to know?"

By the end of the meeting, the president, impressed but still skeptical, requested to arrange a trip to our factory to see it all in person. Such stunning and quality products being made here in Uganda? And by a bunch of *girls*, no less? He had to see it to believe it. A few weeks later, an entourage of black SUVs arrived unannounced at our factory, and Agnes gave him a tour of our operations, showing him just what's possible when women are given the opportunity not just to survive but *thrive*.

A few months later and halfway across the globe, I sat in the darkened theatre of the Kennedy Center in Washington, DC, and listened as the First Ladies Laura Bush and Michelle Obama introduced a short film starring Agnes. There on the glowing screen, as hundreds of African dignitaries and U.S. politicians watched, Agnes explained, with the same gentle but direct and matter-of-fact tone I had come to know and love, the issues facing women in her community and the reality *she* refused to accept. She shared about her work with Sseko and her dream to create a place where women know they are valued, held to high expectations, and given the opportunity to become the leaders they were created to be. When the video ended, I listened with tears streaming down my face as MICHELLE FREAKING OBAMA sat in an inspired awe and said of Aggie, "A portrait of the Modern African Woman. She is the future. Where she leads, we will follow."

A girl from the village, who was almost traded for cattle, making waves with political royalty, here and there.

Agnes currently serves as the general manager of our company and co-chair of our board. She and I often reminisce and laugh about that first fateful tea date between two idealistic and ambitious women in their early twenties with their Big Dreams and Very Important Ideas.

The principled journalist running a fashion brand, and the UN-bound academic overseeing one of the largest manufacturing companies in Uganda.

"What a surprise," Aggie says about her could-never-have-seen-it-coming career trajectory. "I wasn't interested in ladies' fashion but I never for a day regretted choosing Sseko over my UN dream."

"But," she muses, "what we're doing here—connecting women in Uganda and America and Ethiopia and India to come together and create a rising tide for all of us—I suppose in a way, we've just created our own *United Nations*."

What a *lovely* surprise.

INTERLUDE

Gulu, Uganda > London, England > Portland, Oregon

A few months after our first son was born we went to visit some of our best friends, who live about an hour outside of London in a quaint, dreamy little village. They graciously offered to watch our son one night so my husband, Ben, and I could take the train into London and have a night in the city to ourselves for the first time since we became parents. Before we even left for England, I spent hours researching what we'd do during our romantic 18-hour getaway. I bought tickets to a play I'd heard wonderful things about and we booked an Airbnb in the heart of the theatre district.

Call me a naive first-time parent, but I was not prepared for the havoc an eight-hour time change would wreak on our chubby, wonderful Tiny Tyrant. Even after several days of getting acclimated to our new time zone, he was not sleeping at all and was only consolable with nursing nearly nonstop through the night. By the time we got to the day of our anticipated mini getaway, it became very clear that our saucy night in the city was turning into a decidedly sauce-less whole family affair.

We had two (pricey) tickets to one of the hottest shows in town and there was obviously no way we could bring a vocally robust baby to the theatre with us. I was devastated.

Since I am the theatre lover, my husband suggested that I go to the show alone and offered to take our son for a little nighttime exploration of the city in the meantime. I was so disappointed that the evening wasn't turning out to be what I had dreamed. I got angry. And then I went and found some pistachio gelato. (Anger then ice cream. Par for my course.)

But after nursing my disappointment for a minute or two, I started asking a question that, after years and years of practice, has become almost instinct to me in times of disappointment and frustration: What tiny miracle is there buried beneath this disappointment?

Pluckies, once you master the art of being open to a good surprise, you can take it one step further and become a *Miracle Hunter*. Miracle Hunters are relentless. And they understand the difference between expectations and being *expectant*. They look for tiny miracles *everywhere* but they stay open to being surprised by *what* exactly that miracle will look and feel like. They have cultivated what I call "Positive Paranoia" and believe that hidden within the disappointment, the failure, the unexpected change of plans, there is a nugget of a miracle just waiting to be discovered.

So, I finished my pistachio gelato, shook off the dust of disappointment and expectations, and let The Miracle Hunt begin. (It helps if you whisper to yourself dramatically, "May the odds be ever in your favor.")

The minute you start hunting for miracles, the entire way you see the world changes.

I wandered down a street in the theatre district about 45 minutes before the show started, and I heard a hauntingly beautiful voice, singing in the distance. I looked up and saw a street performer playing his guitar and singing into the crisp November night. Propped up on his guitar case was a cardboard sign that said he had just arrived from South Korea. I listened to him sing and play for just a few moments before a shopkeeper came out and asked him to leave, mid-song. He politely obliged and started packing up his things in a rush as the shopkeeper looked on.

I'm not sure I realized it until right then, but street performers have a special place in my heart. I think it is because they are such an obvious example of someone who is not waiting for an invitation or permission. They don't rely on the gatekeepers of venues or radio stations to tell them they are good enough. They just do the thing they were created to do.

When I saw this brave soul get asked to leave his spot on the corner, I thought about how commonplace that experience must be for him. Here he is trying to put his gift out into the world, and time and time again he gets ignored and rejected and passed by. But, no doubt, he will find another street corner and he will keep playing. That's how true and important his song is. He will create and he will do the hard and brave work of putting that creation out into the universe regardless of how it is received.

Watching him pack up, I knew this was a clue. My heart started racing as I walked toward him to invite him to come to the play with me. I was clearly caught up in the thrill of The Miracle Hunt.

Of course, there was the risk that I would be rejected by this perfect stranger. There was a risk that he would be a total weirdo and it would make for an incredibly awkward evening and ruin my one night out in London doing one of the things I love to do most.

There is *always* risk, Traveler. But the great myth is that we can make decisions and traverse paths that have less risk than others. It sounds like common sense. The trodden path is the safe one and the unmarked trail is perilous.

But this is a lie.

The tentacles of this lie have grown like insidious vines so deep into the heart of humans that many of us accept it as absolute and complete commonsense fact.

But *every* path, *every* decision, *every* lifestyle has risks.

No matter if you choose to "play it safe" or go a little out of your comfort zone, each path has a unique set of risks. When you become someone who hunts for miracles, the risks are indeed a little different than if you always stay within your comfort zone.

But after you've hunted and caught enough miracles, the Old Risks of embarrassing yourself, getting hurt, making a mistake, looking like a weirdo, or getting into a little bit of trouble start to *pale* in comparison to the Newly Realized Risk of missing the miracles that are out there waiting for you. You become more aware and afraid of the Newly Realized Risks that come with living a "comfortable" and "safe" life that might keep you from disappointment or failure but that also keep you from a life of *wonder*. You risk missing out on growing into who you were created to be and you risk missing out on the chance to be utterly surprised and delighted by what makes you come alive. You miss out on the possibility of experiencing the joy and wonder that comes when you see how your living out loud can inspire others to do the same.

I knew in the midst of the disappointment of our ruined evening there was a miracle waiting for me, and I was desperately afraid to miss it.

So I introduced myself to the street performer and asked if he had any interest in accompanying me to the theatre. I told him about my husband and son and explained that I had an extra ticket and that I was pretty certain that all along the ticket actually belonged to him and that I was so grateful I found the rightful owner before the show began! Imagine the luck!

After I excitedly and nervously extended the invitation, Ji Sung looked at me quizzically for a moment without saying anything, and I realized that I forgot to actually ask if he even spoke English before I launched into my miracle spiel. But after an initial silence and confused stare, his eyes got wide and he said *yes*. Not only did he accept my invitation, but he went on to tell me that his *entire life* he had wished to see a play but that he had never been to one before. Not even an amateur play! Tonight was the night! London has some of the best theatre in the entire world and this particular show was *laden* with accolades. His inaugural theatre experience would be the *crème de la crème*.

We walked together a few blocks down Shaftesbury Avenue to the Gielgud Theatre. We were quite the sight, the two of us, toting his music stand and amp and guitar down the busy cobblestone street. Luckily, the theatre had a storage room, and after some explaining, they graciously allowed us to store what amounted to a small truckload of musical apparatus during the show.

There is something magical about the theatre for me. But I will say, the magic increased tenfold as I sat beside someone who was absolutely entranced, seeing this particular brand of magic unfold for the first time. On more than one occasion, I looked over to see tears rolling down Ji Sung's cheek. After the show, we sat in our seats as the theatre emptied. I asked him what he thought of the show and how it made him feel. With tears still in his eyes, he shared with me that his family back in South Korea had essentially disowned him because of his desire to build a career in music and art. After he declared that he didn't want to pursue a more traditional "respectable" professional path, his parents would no longer support him. After a heartbreaking season of conflict with his family, he decided he needed to leave South Korea for a while and try his hand at becoming a career artist. London was his first stop and he had just arrived a few days ago. And he was beginning to question his decision. The city was so new and overwhelming. He was so alone. Was it all worth it? Was pursuing this dream of being a musician and getting to create art for a living worth the *incredibly* high cost?

The show we had just seen, *The Curious Incident of the Dog in the Night-Time*, was the story of a 15-year old boy with autism who sets out on a perilous adventure to solve a mystery and find his mother. As the boy travels into London by himself, he is completely overwhelmed by the sheer size and stimuli of the city. But despite all odds, he persists in his mission and eventually succeeds. Ji Sung told me, sitting there in that now nearly empty theatre, that this was the story he needed at the moment he needed it. It was a clear sign for him to just *keep going*.

Seeing this very story played out in front of him at this very moment in his journey was his miracle. Getting to sit beside Ji Sung as he witnessed the magic of the theatre for the first time was *mine*.

I never saw or spoke to Ji Sung again. Sometimes miracles start and end in the course of minutes or hours. But the residue of those miracles is what slowly changes us from having expectations to being expectant. Here is my fair warning: once you start hunting for miracles, you can't stop. It's highly addictive, this business. You start expecting them. You learn to stop expecting *what* that miracle will look like or *how* it will feel, you just start to believe that the miracle is out there, waiting for you to find it.

Seek and ye shall find, Pluckies.

EIGHT

Get Your Steps In

So here I was in Uganda with a brand-spanking-new harebrained idea. From charity to chicken farm, why not strappy sandals next?

I was now on my third attempt at solving this Really Juicy Problem and I have to say, my confidence in this particular idea was pretty low. Manufacture sandals that we can sell in the U.S. that will enable girls to stay in school?

I had NO IDEA where to start.

I Googled it.

FAIL.

I looked around for someone else doing something similar.

FAIL.

None. Nada. Nothing.

At the time, I was staying in a basement "guesthouse." I paid $7 a night for a room with a bunk bed that, in addition to me, was occupied by a rotating cast of characters traveling through Uganda. I'd stay up too late every night ideating about my Strategic Plan and then I would wake up each morning to the sound of the world's most obnoxiously loud birds and lie underneath my mosquito net with a truly paralyzing sense of *dread*.

I still did not have a plan and I had no idea where to start.

I had an entire day to fill, and the emptiness of that day spread out ahead of me every morning was horrifying and daunting because all it did was amplify the fact that I had no idea HOW to take the first step toward making this dream a reality.

So, I'd "think" and "research" and "talk" a little more about my idea and eventually get distracted with the tiny tasks that can so easily fill our days and occupy our minds but never result in much of anything. At the end of every day, as "busy" as I was, I felt like a big, fat failure.

Because here is the thing: we can become so afraid and overwhelmed at not knowing what the *Right* First Step is that we fall into fear-induced stillness.

I eventually got so fed up at not knowing what the Almighty First Step was that I *finally* just decided that my first step would simply be . . . *getting my steps in*. Think about having a Fitbit for your life. Doesn't actually matter where you're going, so much as that you get your steps in.

While I can't give you a map or tell you what your first step should be, I *can* share with you a deal I made with myself that *changed everything*.

And while this exact deal didn't result in a 12-step, foolproof, PowerPoint-worthy strategic plan, it saved my little dream and it propelled me down a path where eventually a fairly decent strategic plan *could* exist in its rightful place and time and purpose.

Let me be clear: I did not discover The *Right* First Step, The *Right* Door, or The *Right* Connection. This deal just propelled me into *movement*. And that movement is what saved me. It's not steps of any kind, in any direction that we should be afraid of. Not even the ones in the exact "wrong" direction. It's fear-induced stillness we should be wary of. Movement is *never fatal*. Steps earnestly and courageously taken toward making your own path will never, ever kill you.* And this deal simply broke my inertia and got me out of my head and into some momentum. It helped me start to get my steps in.

About this deal: it was not just a fleeting thought that I said to myself in the shower. I'm no self-control guru, so if it's not written down or spoken out loud with some kind of accountability, as soon as something gets a teeeeeeeeensy bit difficult I'm all like, "Wait *what*? Who *me*? I don't think I ever said *that*. I'm outie!"

Given this respectable and charming character trait, I am a big fan of making actual, written contracts with myself. So, I whipped up this little legally (in my mind) binding agreement to complete the World's Easiest Goal designed to simply get me moving and taped it to my hostel wall above the bed.

Starting today, every day for the next two weeks, you will wake up with the sun.† You will brush your teeth, wash your pits, and gather your things, and you will walk out your hostel door. You will board a taxi van and you will ride that van until the end of the line. And then you will get out of the van and wander around downtown Kampala,

---

*Metaphorically. You could, of course, actually die in the process of pursuing your dreams. I have come close on multiple occasions. But you can also die driving 70MPH down the highway to a job you hate so . . . you choose.

†Luckily, the sun doesn't rise until just before 7 in Uganda. Not trying to break a sweat or impress anyone here, people.

asking questions and following leads. You will not stop asking questions.

You will not, under any circumstances in the next two weeks, concern yourself with the BIG PICTURE, the STRATEGIC PLAN, the HOW or the VERY IMPRESSIVE BIG DREAM. You will simply put one foot in front of another. Ask questions. Follow leads.

You will do these things each day, all day, and you will not come home until sunset. You will simply get in your steps.

Best Regards,

Elizabeth Ashley Forkin

Traveler, I understand that there is a good chance you are not a 22-year-old, unemployed, single woman paying $7 a night for her living quarters and able to wander aimlessly through a foreign country for two weeks to fulfill such "A Deal." But do *not* use this as an excuse, because the specifics of *my* deal is not the point here. The point is this: the deal I made with myself was *well within my abilities* during this season of life. The deal did not rely on luck or the right connection or permission from someone else or anything else we are tempted to blame for our lack of movement. It was an agreement that a ten-year-old child of average intelligence or an exceptionally bright and well-trained monkey could have done with a relative amount of ease and notable lack of existential angst. *But I wouldn't have actually done it if I hadn't written it down.* And there's a good chance that without a written deal in place, you won't either.

The deal wasn't about a specific outcome, it was intended to break my inertia and *get me moving*.

I'm happy to report that I fulfilled the terms of my agreement. For two weeks, I wandered, asking questions and following leads. Most of which were dead ends. But regardless, I got my steps in.

One day, I decided a good first step would be to find a leather supplier, given that the sandals I was envisioning were made of... leather. Surely it wouldn't be too difficult. Through my chicken farming stint, I learned how incredibly important agriculture is in the Ugandan economy with over 70 percent of Ugandan families engaged in livestock rearing.[1] But for the life of me, I couldn't find a source for *leather*. I wandered around downtown asking about this quandary until I finally met someone who seemed eager to help. His name was Joseph and he spoke very little English,* but luckily the universal language of Old MacDonald knows no cultural boundaries and when I *mooed* at him to help paint the picture of what I was looking for, his eyes lit up.

Joseph told me he knew *exactly* where I could find this mysterious material and proceeded to lead me clear to the other side of town. It took us two hours of weaving our way through traffic and open-air-market stalls to get to the destination, which was plenty of time for me to conjure up lots of fantastical images that looked like something out of a "Behind the Scenes" magazine spread in a J.Crew catalog. I envisioned a charming little shop with floor-to-ceiling shelves lined with buttery-soft samples of leather swatches in every color of the Pantone Rainbow. A portly old man would emerge from behind the shop wearing a canvas apron with pockets holding antique leatherworking tools and he'd teach me everything I needed to know about the finest techniques in leather shoe-making.

*Although his English was much better than my Luganda.

When we finally arrived, I was sunburned and dehydrated and completely out of Luganda small-talk phrases, but none of that mattered because I had FINALLY CRACKED THE CODE AND FOUND THE GOLDEN EGG. Joseph was my guardian angel and he was leading the way to The Promised Land.

Only, when we pushed open the rusty steel door to the market stall and walked in, I found myself surrounded by huge slabs of beef hanging from giant hooks. As I looked up at Joseph, desperately confused, he dramatically motioned his arms, stepped back, and slightly bowed as if revealing his masterpiece while he made eye contact with me and said gleefully, "See, sister! Mooooooooooooo!"

That was the first of many epic, pathetic dead ends. But, as demoralizing as they were, my two weeks were not up. So, the next day, I woke up, boarded the van, and didn't go home until sunset.

I got my steps in.

Looking back, there was not a single connection, relationship, material, or supplier that I discovered in those first two weeks that is relevant in my business and life today. But you know what I did find during those two weeks? I found the first link. And the first link led to the next. And without a doubt, had I not discovered that first crappy link, I wouldn't have discovered the second less crappy link which eventually lead me to the fourteenth kinda decent link which was what I needed to actually move forward in the *general direction of north*.

I didn't get to skip the first, small, misled, Bless Your Heart, waste-of-time steps in the "wrong" direction. And you don't get to skip them either, Pluckies.

I can't tell you what your first step is because here is the terrible and wonderful truth: you are entirely and completely unique and so is your path. You and your path are made up of every moment of every conversation you've had. Everything that's broken your heart. Every suture that's helped stitch that shattered heart back together and every crack that still exists. Every idea you've had, every person you've loved, every trip you've taken. Every neighborhood you've ever lived in and every family member who has loved you and disappointed you and every inside joke that makes you laugh until you cry at the most socially unacceptable times. *All of it* culminates with you and in YOU. There is no one else who sees the world quite like you do. And where you are going, no one has ever been before. Because that's the terror and the beauty of The Path, Traveler. It's *only made by walking.*

You've got to stop asking for directions to a place that doesn't yet exist. There is no Right First Step. There are only the sacred steps that will make your path.

But only if you walk it.

* * *

When I came back to the U.S., I realized that in order to sell enough sandals to send three girls to college I needed to get the word out and get these sandals onto store shelves. I had *zero* concept about how one goes about getting their products in a store. Turns out we didn't learn about that in journalism school. Up until that point in my life, I kind of thought stuff just magically appeared on shelves for me to look at and try on. I had truly not given a second thought to how it got there. I knew nothing of trade shows and sales reps and buyers and purchase terms. I didn't know the first step to take.

So instead of somehow magically waiting to figure it out via research or some fortuitous connection, one day, completely ignorant and unprepared, I walked into a little boutique in my neighborhood with nothing more than a pair of sandals on my feet and a pair in my hands. I asked the lady behind the counter if the store owner was in, and she nodded and pointed to a woman arranging some clothes in the back corner of the store. I thanked her and walked over to the lady with her back turned toward me and said as confidently as I could muster, "Excuse me?" When she turned around, before she had a chance to say a word, I launched into what could have been my audition tape for a terrible QVC infomercial. Looking back, pitching a store owner in the middle of her store in the middle of shopping hours was inappropriate and ill-advised on so many levels, but how was I to know?

I wasn't. I didn't know it then, but the point of this first step wasn't actually to win the account. The point was to get one step closer to learning how one wins accounts.

When I finally finished my sales pitch, the woman looked at me and most likely in an act of desperation to just get me out of her store, she said, "If you want to leave your card and line sheets at the counter, I'd be happy to take a closer look later and I'll let you know if we're interested."

LINE SHEETS.

I knew what a line was.

I knew what sheets were.

I had ZERO idea of what the combination of these words meant in the context I had just heard them.

Zero.

Nada.

Jibberish.

So, I looked right at her and said, "Oh! The *line sheets*! I can't believe I forgot the *line sheets*! I just need to go grab the *line sheets* from my office and I'll be back before the store closes with the *line sheets*," saying *line sheets* entirely too many times for it not to seem suspicious and obvious that I was absolutely in over my head.

I went outside and got in my 1999 Mazda Protege and while still sitting in the parking lot of that boutique, I got on my Blackberry and typed in "Boutique store retail line sheet what is it?" into the search engine.

And, as usual, Mama Google pulled through for me. I learned that a "line sheet" is basically Retail 101. It is essentially a stripped-down catalog of all your products with photos, pricing, and product information.

I called my best friend who was fun-employed at the time and we did the jankiest photoshoot you've ever seen, featuring the sandals and our stunning array of four different-colored strap options on the sidewalk outside of my apartment.

I quickly uploaded the photos, added pricing information and our logo. I ran to Office Depot where I printed out five color copies (I wanted to seem legit so I made five copies. Look, I AM SO LEGIT AND WELL RESOURCED THAT I HAVE EXTRA COPIES IF YOU NEED THEM! Love me, please.) and managed to get back to the boutique to drop off the line sheets by their 7 PM close time, acting cool as a cucumber.

Oh, *these old things?*

And with that we actually, miraculously landed our first-ever wholesale account. But more importantly, I learned what a line sheet was and that standard wholesale pricing is about 50 percent of retail pricing and that SKU stood for Stock Keeping Unit. And I say miraculous because in the years of building our wholesale business that followed, it usually took about five or six "nos" for every "yes." But as Mark Cuban, who would later go on to give me a big fat NO on national television, says, "Every no gets me closer to a yes.")

You can spend days, weeks, months, even *years* hemming and hawing over what the *best* first step is. Or, you can just take a step. Any step! A shot in the dark. That shot in the dark will, at the very least, give you a clue as to what the *next* step is. Which still might not be THE BEST step, but why does that matter? A step in any direction is infinitely better than standing in fear-induced stillness.

You don't need a map that reveals exactly where you're going. What you need is a better, stronger, maybe slightly louder and bossier *compass*. An inner compass that you can hear over the cacophony of the millions of voices and neon lights shouting THIS WAY! You need to build a compass that will keep you walking in the general direction of True North.

So, starting *right now*, make a deal with yourself and then *keep your word*. The terms of the deal don't matter: that it gets you moving—in any direction—does. Wake up. Wash your pits. Follow the leads and ask the questions and take some steps down the path you're making *by walking it*.

NINE

Get Hooked on Making (and Keeping!) Promises

After months of wandering through the markets (and roadside butcher shops) in Uganda and sustaining multiple shallow wounds while attempting to hand-make leather sandals at 3 AM in a poorly lit room, I knew it was time to make a promise.

Why a promise? Because I knew myself well enough to know that if I were to leave Uganda and go back home to the U.S. without making some kind of promise, that this little sandal idea would get filed away with virtually every other "great" idea or midnight dream that seems silly and naive and impossible in the light of day. And while I didn't know *how* to deliver on the promise, I did know that I desperately didn't want this dream to suffer that fate.

Promises can push us one step beyond where we'd naturally stop and throw in the towel.

I am 100 percent, absolutely confident that not only my business but also the very thing that propelled me out of aimlessness and toward building a life of passion and purpose would not have happened had I not made a very serious promise that I had *zero* idea how I was going to keep.

I met with the leaders of the girls' school and I pitched them my (third) little idea. It checked *their* boxes of keeping the girls together, learning a skill, and earning money for college. They were all in. Finally, an idea that didn't suck!

Knowing that the headmistress was obviously much more familiar with the students of her school than I was, I asked her to choose the first three young women. She met with all the teachers and together they decided on three women who were ridiculously smart and showed incredible leadership potential, but who also came from particularly challenging backgrounds.

Their names were Mary, Mercy, and Rebecca.

I had met each of these girls at one point or another during my time at the school, and I requested to meet with all three of them together after their last class of the day. We sat under the now iconic (at least in our world) mango tree in front of the school's meeting hall, and I tried not to show how terrified and unsure I was about what was about to happen.

I showed Mary, Mercy, and Rebecca a few samples of the sandals I made, and I told them my (threadbare) plan for how we'd make more of them. I presented them with the almighty "Manufacturing Guide," which was a three-ring binder filled with hand-drawn templates of sandals size 5–11 with measurements on where to cut the leather and where to punch the holes where the fabric ribbons would lace through.

And then I made my promise: "If you promise to make these sandals for the next nine months, I will go back home to the

U.S. and sell every last one of them and I *promise* that all three of you will earn enough money to go to college next fall."

No exceptions or stipulations based on circumstances outside of my control. After all, I felt like if I was going to ask them to trust me enough to spend nine months sitting on a patch of grass making sandals, the least I owed them was a serious commitment to what they'd get out of the deal. It felt like a huge, scary stretch, but I chose three women (instead of say, fifteen) because I figured that if I absolutely fell on my face with the sandal gig, I had a year to beg, plead, and fund-raise to scrape together the money needed to send them to college. (And I *really* didn't want to have to do that.)

Either through slinging sandals or begging on a street corner, I would keep my promise to them.

But it was also, and perhaps more importantly, a promise I made *to myself*. I didn't know a lot, but I knew enough to know that the next year of my life would probably bring its fair share of doubts and struggles and moments where it would be awfully easy to let that silly, idealistic dream I had in a far-off place become a distant and maybe even nostalgic, bless-your-heart memory.

So, I said it out loud. I implicated other people in my dream and didn't give myself a way out.

As my friend Robert Frost would say:*

I can see no way out but through.[1]

If you're following the principles of Beginner's Pluck to build a life of passion and impact, you're going to reach a

---

*I admit to using the term *friend* rather loosely.

crossroads (sooner than you think) when it will be time to *make the promise.*

The point of making a promise is that it's incredibly powerful to say something out loud. The moment we go from "in our heads" to "spoken into existence" the game changes. There is a new level of commitment and gravity that is exactly the ingredient you need to get your butt in gear. You will not build a life of purpose and impact with "I'll try," "Maybe later," or "We'll see." You will not build it with quiet, silent hopes that never see the light of day. So, write them down and say them out loud.

Honest Abe[2] said that discipline is "choosing between what you want now and what you want most." This is a great way to think about the promises you make. Think less about what you want to do this Friday night (Netflix always, duh) and more about living a life that will reveal and refine who you were truly created to be. Then, make a promise that aligns not with what you want *now*, but what you want *most* in life.

Building a life of purpose and impact is not some mystical, cryptic, cosmic code to be cracked, it's actually just a series of meaningful promises, small and large, that *you actually keep.* So make the promise. And then lock the back door and shoot out the glowing EXIT sign with the BB gun your gramps gave you on your eighth birthday and Do. The. Work.

No way out but through, Traveler.

✳ ✳ ✳

In the year that followed, I was laser focused on that Very Important Promise (VIP) and in the years since have realized that making and keeping Very Important Promises is a nonnegotiable in building a life of purpose, passion, and impact.

However, we only have limited plucks, er, promises to give. We *must* make them wisely and they've got to be *good* promises. What I mean by *good* is that they need to align with our vision for life and they need to set us up for success.

In an effort to move us out of theory and into practicality, I'll share with you how I make and keep Very Important Promises, not just in my business but in every area of my life.

1. I start with my dreams and craft a *single sentence* vision statement that synthesizes the highest-level dream I have for that specific area of life. I have five vision statements that cover the areas of life that matter most to *me*: Personal Growth, Marriage, Parenting, Vocation, and Community. Together, these five vision statements make up what I believe would be a well-lived life of purpose and impact *for me.* Your vision statement should be something that you can see being just as relevant ten years from now as it is today. Lives of purpose and impact are not built overnight, and your vision should have longevity to support this truth. Once you've crafted your vision statement for each of the most important areas of your life, you can combine them into a single Life Manifesto. (I mean, who wants to go another second of living WITHOUT A PERSONAL MANIFESTO?)

2. Then, beneath each vision statement, I make a series of specific Very Important Promises that serve to support my vision statement and that I evaluate once a quarter. The fewer the better, but it is *very* important that your supporting promises are SMART, which

according to business and management guru George Duran[3] stands for:

Specific. The more specific the better! It's a pain up front but will give you the clarity you need to be successful.

Measurable. It's not ambiguous or subjective. You either did it or you didn't.

Actionable and Achievable. Your promises should be *within your capabilities*. They also need to be within *your* control. You cannot always control your circumstances. You *can* control your response.

Relevant. The terms of the promise need to support your vision statement. You only get to make a few promises, so the ones you make need to matter.

Time-bound. Your circumstances and capabilities are ever evolving. Your promises should reflect this reality. You should expect to evaluate, adjust, and reestablish your promises at *pre-determined* intervals.

For instance, "Be a great mom" is *not* a SMART promise. It's vague and subjective, and if you don't define "Great Mom" *explicitly* and *for yourself,* you'll feel the weight of everyone else's definition clumped together in a big, weighty, ambiguous blob that won't even align with your vision statement and will leave you feeling like a failure nearly all the time.

Instead, an example of one of my Parenting VIPs is, "Model healthy relationships by engaging in honest marital reconciliation in front of the boys, being intentionally affectionate with one another and *always* speaking positively about Ben when he is not around, *even* when I am frustrated or hurt."

The process of defining *your* vision and *your* promises that will support that vision will take time and intentionality, but your return on investment will be a beautiful life lived *on purpose.*

⁂ ⁂ ⁂

Defining your vision statements and making Very Important Promises is going to be *critical* to your success, because once you courageously embark on the journey of building a life of purpose and impact, you are all but inviting the most powerful force to sabotage you from this good, juicy, life-giving work. Before you even take the first step, you will be tempted to start BSing (Busy and Should) your way out of it. Here's how to combat that.

Busy:

I challenge you to a 30-day experiment: every time you're tempted to say "I'm too busy" say instead, "That's not a priority for me, therefore it's not a promise I've made and I'll have to decline." If you're brave enough to make the switch, one of two things is going to happen when you do:

Either you're going to feel *really bad* when you realize that something that *deeply* matters to you (your kids, your health, your marriage, your commitment to justice, cultivating life-long friendships) isn't *actually* the priority you want to believe it is. This will compel you to go back to your Very Important Promises and see what you can cut in order to create space for the things that *really* matter to you.

OR

Saying that statement may initially sting because we've been conditioned to feel bad about "Nos," but as the words settle, it will feel *true* to you. Instead of allowing this thing you're "too busy for" to perpetually hang over your head, your NO (because it is not a priority or promise) will free you up to unapologetically and confidently spend your limited moments and resources on the things that matter *most* to you.

The year after making my first Very Important Promise to Mary, Mercy, and Rebecca, I said "NO" so many times to so many things in order to keep that Very Important Promise. Ten years later, I can't remember a single one of those "Nos," even the ones that I know stung in the moment, because they didn't matter as much as keeping that promise did. In hindsight, there is not a thing I regret missing out on, because keeping that one Very Important Promise changed *everything*. Ten years later, I'm a wife and mom and entrepreneur and my Very Important Promises look quite a bit different than they did back then, but one thing has remained: I still have to say no in order to say YES! to the things that matter most.

Getting good at saying no doesn't make you a monster. It makes you a maker, keeper, and defender of your good promises and will enable you to build a life you love.

Should:

Once you actually take the time and intention to write down your promises, every time you come across something you think you *should* be doing that gives you a pang of guilt or shame, you can quickly run it through *your* Very Important Promises. Is this "Should" something *I* considered important enough to include in the limited promises I have to give? If the answer is no, either:

1. You shake it off because it's not currently a part of *your* promise and therefore it does not apply to *you*. You

take solace in your list of Very Important Promises and move on.

2. You find this particular Should a prospect worth considering, and you make a note to evaluate it at your *next* Very Important Promise review but *not before then.* You can't just let Shoulds hit the fan willy nilly, Pluckie! If a Should is real and true and important, it will still be there next quarter.

When you do the work up front to make your Very Important Promises, they will protect you from the flaming bags of Should that will inevitably land on your proverbial front step.

The most important thing to understand is that other people's Shoulds have no place in building a life of impact and purpose. You are the maker of Good Promises and the landlord of your own brain. So, if you want to get to a place where you can make and keep important promises that will propel you toward building a life of purpose and impact, let's stop messing around and kick the Should out of it, shall we?

* * *

A decade ago, I made a promise to three young women because I truly believed in the depth of my soul that our world would be a little better and brighter if *they* were at the helm. It was a pretty big promise. But I needed a big promise to fuel me because the year that followed was not exactly the unicorns and rainbows I'd grown to assume "Finding Your Passion" would entail.

Four days after I got home from Uganda for the first time, my now-husband, Ben, proposed. As he was down on one knee, I was contemplating if I needed to disclose my financial commitment to these three young women in Uganda before he consented to a legal union and a shared bank account. Very romantic, I know.

Five months later, instead of settling into life together and playing house and occasionally fighting about who was supposed to do the dishes, Ben and I were exhausted, poor newlyweds fighting over our corporate structure while all our neighbors heard us screaming at each other about our company finances (or lack thereof) in the apartment parking lot. The first time I left for a long trip to Uganda, just a few months after our wedding, we held each other and cried in the airport parking garage like a couple of dramatic teenagers who just got Montague and Capulet-ed. Later that year, *the week after* Ben quit his day job and we lost our health insurance, I had an incredibly stressful leukemia scare. (Turns out it was dormant malaria. #workperks.) For most of that year, I was really lonely working all day in our apartment by myself and staying up until wee hours of the morning for daily Skype calls with our team in Uganda. Ben would come home from his day job only to work on Sseko until we both fell asleep with packaging supplies and sandals covering every inch of our bedroom floor. Our biggest shipment ever got delayed *for three months* at the port in Mombasa, Kenya. Customers were cancelling their orders left and right because of the delay. Turns out the container had a leak and so for months our precious sandals sat in a giant hot, damp, dark metal box. By the time they finally arrived in the U.S., *hundreds* of sandals were covered in fuzzy white mold. We thought we were done for. For days and days, Ben and I sat in silence in the 100-degree heat of a Kansas City summer with toothbrushes and bleach water, faces smeared with dust and sweat, looking like a couple of seriously depressed chimney sweeps, barely speaking a word to one another while we attempted to save those sandals, and our business and dream, from a moldy, deadly fate.

I *promise* you that if I hadn't made a promise, I would have waved the white (moldy) flag.

But then? In the midst of the bleary-eyed impossibility of actually keeping the promise?

We did it.

We sold enough sandals to send Mary, Mercy, and Rebecca to college. Our friend Tyler went out to the girl's school to deliver the news to them in person, and he took a grainy, sideways video of them cheering and crying and hugging one another and sent it to us. We must have watched it one thousand times. We also cheered, cried, and made out for a while and then walked down to McCoy's Pub to celebrate with baked mac & cheese. Before we even got the bill for the celebratory meal we could barely pay for, we started dreaming about the *next* promise we could make.

We were officially *hooked* on making promises and actually keeping them.

The last ten years has been a series of small and mundane and outrageous and scary promises to help fulfill that very first promise and every promise since. In fact, this entire journey has been a long, weaving domino-string of promises that we didn't quite know how we were going to keep. And with every promise fulfilled, we became more hooked on making and keeping meaningful ones.

Promises are a way of tying us back to those magic moments in time when, before it got really difficult, we believed that our dream was actually possible. A promise is hope with a timeline and accountability. So, write it down and get specific. An articulated vision for our lives and the promises that support it will help ward off our excuses so we can get on with the magic of making and keeping good promises—promises that will call out the truest parts of who we are and who we want to be.

TEN

Be Good with Good Enough

had made a promise I didn't know how I was going to keep. I had promised Mary, Mercy, and Rebecca that I would go back to the U.S. and sell enough sandals to send them to college. I was in *deep*. I didn't have a plan. I certainly didn't have organized or robust systems in place. To be completely honest, I wasn't even proud of the product. These subpar, rough around the edges (literally) sandals were a pretty far cry from what I imagined when I began this saga. I knew they could be better, but not without significantly more investment in higher quality raw materials and proper tools. For now, we were doing the best we could with scissors and scraps.

The supply chain.

The plan.

The budget. (Or lack thereof.)

The product itself.

It all felt shaky and subpar.

And then.

Something really, really wonderful happened.

I feel pretty confident that had this event not occurred, my little dream probably would have never gotten the wings it needed to finally take flight.

Close your eyes for a second and just imagine at this point in the story, the best possible thing that could happen to launch this idea out of Dream Orbit and into reality.

It was so fortuitous.

I am eternally grateful for this piece of sheer good luck that happened to me.

> Better than finding out my grandpa was an expert sandal cobbler back in his day and could teach me everything I needed to know.
>
> Better than getting an investor to back the idea.
>
> Better than being on *Oprah*. (Sorry, Queen!)

Are you ready for it?

I ran out of time and I ran out of money.

I knew deep down that all of it—the product, the supply chain, the model, the quality, the brand—all of it could be better, but I simply didn't have the money or the time.

Every penny I had saved since my middle school babysitting days had been spent on this adventure. First, there was the flight and a visa and the shots and all the completely useless REI gear. Then there were the hostel fees and the bus rides and food. And right around the time that I thought maybe I would have found a job or perhaps a volunteer position that would at least earn me a stipend of some kind, I started really burning through my budget by purchasing yards and yards of fabric and leather hides and plastic crates to keep our supplies organized. My last $100, that I had planned on covering a few more weeks of living expenses, was spent instead on a pedal-powered Singer sewing machine to sew fabric straps for these funky, strappy sandals I designed.

And then the Almighty Moolah was *gone*.

You know what running out of money in the midst of your dream feels like?

Really crappy.

I felt frustrated and demoralized that I had a vision that was *so far* from being executed in the way I envisioned because I just didn't have the resources to bring it to life the way I saw it when I closed my eyes. What I didn't know at the time was that the "You Do Not Have Sufficient Funds to Complete This Withdrawal" message was actually *exactly* what I needed at the *exact* time I needed it.

Dare I say, a miracle?

I didn't need more resources. I didn't need more cobbler expertise. I didn't need more time for planning or perfecting or researching or prototyping because although I desperately wanted all of those things, I didn't actually *need* perfection.

As Voltaire said, "Best is the enemy of good."[1]

And, Pluckies, good enough is usually . . .

Well, good enough.*

* * *

In the very early days of our business when we were still living out of our car, I had the chance to spend a week with

---

*If you are a neurosurgeon, please take this section with a grain of salt. In fact, go ahead and skip ahead to the next chapter, because we're actually going to need you to shoot for perfection. But if you're not a neurosurgeon, this is for you.

Seth Godin and ten other brilliant entrepreneurs, many of whom remain close friends to this day.* During that week-long course, Seth spent a lot of time talking about the myth of preparation, and his teaching changed the course of my business (and life). We're told our whole lives that the more time we spend prepping and preparing, the better the outcome will be. But Seth proposes that unless you absolutely need to be an expert and you're actually willing to put in decades of work to get to Expert Status, you should "Just do the beginner stuff and stop screwing around. Make it good enough and ship it."[2]

But we *love* Preparation Land. We vacation and eventually buy timeshares in Preparation Land because there we have permission to spend one more hour, day, month, or year *not* taking the leap. Preparation Land is comfortable and safe and the schools are great. In Preparation Land, no one criticizes your idea because it's still behind the curtain, getting tinkered on endlessly. Your dream (and your identity) is safe in the bubble of preparation that you've carefully constructed to keep your dream from being poked and prodded and exposed to the harsh elements of the Real World.

But Pluckies, those scary elements won't destroy your dreams. In fact, far from being negative forces that need to be carefully guarded against, those harsh elements are nuggets of *pure gold*. The encouraging feedback *and* the criticism,

*How'd I get that incredible opportunity? I read about the opportunity online and thought to myself "I want that so bad," and so I applied through an application on his website, like everyone else. Perhaps not like everyone else, I was living in my car at the time and applied while pirating Wi-Fi in a McDonald's parking lot somewhere between San Francisco and L.A. before I had any idea how I'd actually get from California to New York if selected for the weeklong program. Apply for the thing. Even if you're living out of your car. You just never know.

the acceptance *and* rejection you'll face when you actually pull back the curtain and finally just *do* the thing will not kill your dream.

It will *refine* it.

If you're grounded and committed to the promise, feedback can make your idea better and stronger and more relevant and robust. You will reach a point in your journey, probably much earlier than you think, where you can't make it better without just putting it to the test. Whatever it is, it doesn't need to be perfect. It just needs to be *good enough for now.*

> So press publish on the post even though you know it could be more witty and articulate.
>
> Make the speech even though your voice still shakes.
>
> Host the dinner party even though you've never cooked for a group before.
>
> Put a fair price tag on the service and then tell your people you're for hire.
>
> Pick up the phone and have the hard conversation even though you don't feel quite ready.
>
> Volunteer for one hour a month even though you wish you could do more.
>
> Share your proposal in the meeting even though you've never led a project.

Start. The. Thing.

I was lucky enough to get forcefully evicted from Preparation Land. Thanks to a dwindling bank account, I knew I had to pack my bags. My only option to keep this frail operation alive was to generate a little cash by selling several hundred sandals that I KNEW could be better.

If selling is hard, selling something you know 100 percent could actually be better is *really* hard.

But the brand!

Our reputation!

My dignity!

Pluckies, do not for a minute assume I didn't have these fears. *Of course* I did.

But my small dream had turned into something big.

I found a problem so interesting, all my other problems started to pale in comparison.

I had gotten my steps in.

I had made a promise I was going to keep.

And, perhaps, most importantly, I was broke as a joke and had no choice but to *do the thing.*

So, I flew back to the U.S. with four suitcases full of very-far-from-perfect strappy leather sandals and I started selling them. I started selling the sandals the only way I knew how: out of the back of my car. (Which is definitely what your parents want you doing with your master's degree in journalism, by the way.)

I wore my sandals every day and God bless any sweet passerby who was stupid enough to compliment me on them. Because doesn't matter where I was—coffee shop, church, grocery store, the middle of a busy crosswalk—I wouldn't let you walk away until you at least tried on a pair of sandals. And handily enough! I kept a pair of sandals *in every single size* in my backpack and more inventory in my trunk at all times.

One day, while caught in completely standstill traffic on the highway, I realized there was a captive audience in our midst. Ben put the car in park and manned the vehicle while I marched myself up and down the freeway shoulder, knocking on the windows of parked cars and asking if I could cheer up any poor souls stuck in traffic purgatory with a pair of hand-crafted sandals for the low, low price of whatever cash they happen to have in their middle console. (Car) Door-to-Door sales at its finest.

How's that for a sophisticated distribution and retail sales strategy?

When I finally decided we needed to figure out a way to sell the sandals using the World Wide Web, we had absolutely zero resources to hire someone to help us build a website. In fact, we were so strapped for cash, I couldn't even afford to buy the book *Building a Web Site for Dummies*, so instead I went to Barnes & Noble, read their copy while still in the store, and built our first website sitting in a fort in the children's section.*

I managed to get the photos of the sandals loaded onto the site but I couldn't figure out how to code an e-commerce experience that could actually accept payment. (This was pre–web shop in a box, people! Kids these days have it so easy. Back in my day . . .) So instead I coded a trick "Add to Cart" button. The trick was, instead of actually adding an item to a cart (which did not exist), when you clicked the Add to Cart button, a dialog box with my cell phone number popped up, instructing the customer to call me so I could take their order over the phone. And ask if they'd like fries with that.

By now you know that I couldn't afford to hire some fancy consultancy to do a focus group to help me really understand consumer perceptions. So instead, I went to The Plaza, the

---

*Which I do realize in hindsight might have been a little creepy for the kids.

busiest shopping area of town and, with sandals and clipboard in hand, I approached complete strangers and would give them one of three "pitches." Then I'd ask them if they would buy the sandals and if so, how much they would pay for them. I compared their answers based off which version of the pitch I gave them. And with this information, I determined our pricing strategy and honed our messaging. You know how much it cost me? Just whatever I spent on a few packages of Imodium, because approaching complete strangers with a clipboard is *no joke you guys*.

In the days since, we've upgraded our website and I no longer require customers to call me at 11 PM to order their sandals. We've *completely* changed our retail model. We've upgraded the product *a lot* and significantly expanded the line. We've changed the messaging, marketing, and pricing strategy. I'm no longer a mule carrying suitcases of sandals through airport security and we've done away with the terrible logo I designed myself on the plane ride back to the U.S. using a really bad font I probably didn't even have the rights to use commercially. *None* of it was perfect. But it was *good enough* to get us going.

If you want to build a life of purpose and impact, I'm afraid you're going to have to get real comfortable with Good Enough. You may have a voice whispering in your ear that you should strive for absolute excellence. That's not your fault, Pluckie! Our entire education system rewards perfection over progress. But know that the magic question you should be asking is, "What is the *least* amount of time/energy/resources I can put into this concept/idea/dream before I can put it out into the universe and actually start getting real-life feedback that will enable me to *make it even better?*"

Excellence is not a requisite for starting. Excellence is something that comes with failure, iteration, and incremental steps forward. And you've got to start somewhere.

So, Traveler, unload that heavy burden of perfection from your pack. And use the extra space to carry a healthy stock of Pepto. You're going to need it.

ELEVEN

Stop, Drop, and WOW

In the early days of Sseko, when my little dream of making sandals that would somehow help enable some of the brightest girls in the country to continue on to college was only weeks old, I'd go for a walk up in the Kololo Hills of Kampala that overlooked the city. I'd dream about creating something that would keep these brilliant young women living life together, earning an income and spurring each other on to greater heights. I dreamed about a day when I could go to that leadership academy and say we could hire not just three women but every. single. girl who wanted to continue her education and become a leader in her community.

I'd whisper WOW when I envisioned the celebration we'd have at the end of each year when we would send these women off to University, speaking life and truth and encouragement over one another. I dreamed about their first day of college. I dreamed about them graduating from college. And then I dreamed about their first day at their first job. I dreamed about how their nerves would wake them before sunrise and how they'd put on the outfit they had picked out the night before, eager to show the world what they had to offer.

I'd whisper WOW when I thought about what it would feel like for her to know that she could say *no* because she was creating her own path and could provide for herself. No to the 40-year-old man who would give her father two cows in exchange for her life. No to the manager at the company who would proposition her for sex in order to get the job.

I'd whisper WOW when I pictured her sending off *her* daughter to school for the first time and about how her daughter's world would be infinitely bigger and filled with more wonder and less fear because of the courageous wake of possibility her mother created for her.

I'd whisper WOW when I imagined all the beautiful things we'd make. I dreamed about traveling around the continent exploring all the unexpected nooks and crannies and following interesting leads. I imagined riding on the back of a motorcycle down a red dirt road, my imagination buzzing with possibility after having just met over coffee and roasted peanuts with artisans who had rich traditions of making beautiful things and dreaming with them about creating something together.

I'd whisper WOW when I closed my eyes and saw a beautiful workshop space of our own, filled with natural light, that was open and well organized with materials from all over the region that would get expertly pieced together to create the most stunning products. I dreamed of our production floor that would buzz with productivity and laughter and creation. I dreamed about the glass-walled offices overlooking the production floor that would have desks and computers, and I dreamed about the women who would sit at those desks, using spreadsheets and purchase orders and production schedules to organize these BIG DREAMS into daily plans.

I had no connections, no supply chain, no answers, and no leads. No idea what the first step was, so all this WOWing felt entirely impossible, of course. But nonetheless, I allowed myself some space away from all of that to let the sense of wonder and possibility grow as I built up my Bank of Wow account before starting to make the withdrawals I'd need to finance the How Plan. I didn't know it at the time, but I was embarking on a lifetime of depositing WOWs and withdrawing HOWs.

* * *

We all know that a dream without a plan is just a wish. But wigging out about not having a Grand Strategic Plan before you *actually need* one is where we lose a lot of good people.

There is a never-ending graveyard of tiny, beautiful dreams that died premature deaths because the dreamer decided they just weren't big enough.

And in that very same graveyard, you'll the find the tragic remains of dreams that somehow made it past the ARE THEY BIG ENOUGH TO MATTER?! gauntlet only to be hacked to a brutal death with a hatchet of *HOW.*

RIP

(Please join me for a moment of silence.)

"But how?!" asked at the wrong time with the wrong sense of importance and urgency is a WMDD.

Weapon of Mass Dream Destruction.

If you find yourself with a fledgling dream and absolutely zero idea of how to help give some wings and legs to that scrawny, delicate thing, let me tell you something:

It's okay.

Take a breath.

This is not a death sentence. In fact, your dream will be well-served by taking up (temporary) residence in the land of WOW, where you truly allow yourself to soak in the utter and complete magic of a really good dream.

Listen, I will be the first to tell you that ideas are a dime a dozen. Even the best ideas don't lead to jack diddle unless the dreaming is backed up with doing and grit and promise keeping. And the people out there building remarkable lives of purpose and passion and impact are *always* the ones who eventually transitioned from the WOW to HOW.

But as true as that is, it doesn't negate the vital importance of the Power of WOW. I am not advocating that we all sit around in La La Land and sing Kum-by-WOW for all of eternity. But first things first, people. And if you want to build a life of purpose and passion, WOW comes before HOW.

Every. Single. Time.

※ ※ ※

Think embracing the Power of WOW is a fluffy, optional task before you move onto the real work of figuring out HOW?

Wrong.

Because here is a brutal truth I need you to know: *no one* else is capable of giving your dream a WOW that is as robust and enthusiastic and wholehearted as you can.

If WOWing your own dreams is a competition, *you* are the Olympic Gold Medalist World Champion of the Universe *by a landslide.*

Your own WOW actually *sets the cap* for how everyone else can and will respond to your dreams. No one, and I mean not your mom, not your spouse, not your super-jazzed-about-life BFF, will *ever* be able *to come close to* your level of enthusiasm you have for your own dreams. You and you alone determine how tall the enthusiasm ceiling is, and everyone forevermore will sit somewhere *below* that ceiling that *you are responsible for setting.*

This is on you. You want people to be excited and committed and sold out on your idea?

Great! Show them the way.

Trying to be nonchalant about your dream or idea because you want to play it cool?

Knock it off.

Now is the time to be VERY CHALANT. If you're sitting around, too cool for school, spit-balling ideas and waiting for someone else to respond to your dream or idea with a level of enthusiasm and WOW that is greater than yours as a signal to keep going? Good luck.

And by good luck I mean, you're in trouble! Because it will *never* happen.

Isn't that exciting?!

You *finally* get to be THE BEST at something! This could be *your* thing! You can be the absolutely number one WOWer of this particular idea, dream, or vision that the world has ever known!

No matter where you are on your journey, dreaming your first BIG Dream or your 100th, you've got to give yourself a little breathing room to say "WOW" and let the magic and the wonder and the awe of the What If?! settle in a bit first. Because there is immense energy that is created during your WOW days, during the days when you let that dream start to grow some wings. And that energy will get you through some cold and lonely nights.

And make no mistake, there will be many of those nights. Many nights of questioning what you're doing and if you're crazy and replaying that conversation a million times in your head desperately wishing you would have said something different. You'll beat yourself up over the wrong decision and you'll doubt yourself more than you ever have. You'll question if you're even worthy of this dream in the first place. The critics will emerge on all sides and you'll want to crumble under the weight of their cowardly, cynical words from the sideline. You'll convince yourself that there is someone else who could do this with more ease and grace and acceptance and success. You'll be tempted to believe the lie that it's already been done and therefore not worth doing. You'll get whiplash from looking to the left and the right and back to the left again to check out your competition and see all the ways in which you suck more than they do.

And during these times, being able to make a withdrawal from a nice, healthy, full bank account of WOW is going to be *critical* to your success.

Like all principles of Beginner's Pluck, having a WOW posture isn't just for the early days. You've got to *constantly* be making deposits into The Bank of Wow because as long as you're growing and challenging yourself, you'll experience doubt and exhaustion and resistance and if you don't have a full WOW account, you'll eventually burn out. You've got to create space to let your imagination run a little wild with ideas and dreams and visions before you bring in the big HOW guns to help you figure it out.

The good news is that if you're a Beginner, WOW is going to come more easily to you! But as you continue on this journey, a spirit of WOW must be intentionally cultivated. This is not fluffy or spontaneous or only when you feel like it. Creating a disciplined spirt of WOW is not the same as daydreaming. It's not about letting your mind wander occasionally when you're stuck at a stoplight or when you take a shower.

A spirit of WOW requires *just as much* commitment and dedication as the HOW will take to implement. No matter where you are in the journey, you have to carve out time and space to let the WOW run a little wild before eventually pulling in the reins and creating an action plan. Today, ten years into this journey, I've got a weekly block on my calendar that just says: "WOW TIME!"

Truly.

WOW TIME is an hour-long time slot where I go for a walk or to a coffee shop and let my WOW run amuck. I don't daydream or let my mind wander. I *vision*. In *vivid color*. I let myself visualize what the future could actually look like. And feel like. And taste like. And sound like.

❉ ❉ ❉

Wherever you are in your journey, you mustn't neglect the importance of making the WOW deposits. I believe in this so much that we've actually made this an official practice in our company.

Inspired by behavioral scientist B. J. Fogg, we have what we call Magic Wand meetings.[1] The entire purpose of these meetings is to create space for WOW and therefore you are actually banned from talking about HOW in these particular meetings. You are not allowed to talk about budgets or constraints or the millions of reasons why something couldn't work. You are only allowed to talk about The Dream.

In order to get you in the WOW mood, you must start out by saying, "If I had a magic wand . . ." and then you get to go wild. Our Magic Wand meetings got *even better* when, after hearing a talk Andy Stanley gave, we implemented a new rule. When you're done with your Magic Wand Statement, there is only one appropriate response from your colleagues: everyone else must actually pause, lean in toward the person who was dreaming out loud, make eye contact with them, and say "WOW." I promise you, forced or not, saying WOW changes the entire spirit of the room and creates a sense of wonder and enthusiasm and possibility. After WOW, the only response your teammates are allowed to give during a Magic Wand meeting is "Yes! And . . ." The greatest comedians and improvisors know that the only way to move a scene or plot forward is to respond to their fellow improv players with "Yes! And . . . ," so that's what we do. We honor their courage and show the Magic Wand holder our willingness to meet them in their dreaming.

Like every principle in this book, this is not just for entrepreneurs. Whether you're dreaming about your family culture or your ministry or your pursuit of your side hustle or art or fitness goals, giving intentional space to WOW your dreams is not optional. And if you're going to let anyone else into your WOW sessions, you need to be militant about the rules of engagement to keep the HOW out. (For now.)

It's also important to note that the necessity of this principle is not limited to the early days of a vision when everything is still a dream. In fact, this practice is just as (if not more!) important to continue as you are further along in your journey, as WOW only gets more difficult. Creating intentional space for WOW is how you ensure that evolution and innovation *continues* to happen. As you build a life of purpose and passion and experience both success and failure, the risks get higher and the Sunk Cost potential gets larger. It becomes increasingly easy to favor "If it ain't broke don't fix it," and to do the safest thing you can imagine to avoid failure.

It's such a natural progression and logical temptation as you grow that getting a little dramatic with an imaginary Magic Wand to regularly snap you out of it and keep you dreaming is quite helpful.

Several years into running our company, we had hit some major milestones. Those WOW dreams that at one time felt *entirely* impossible had been accomplished. We were doing millions of dollars in sales and creating opportunity for hundreds of women in East Africa. Our goal of all local leadership in Uganda was accomplished with an incredible Ugandan management team running a best-in-class manufacturing company. We were no longer operating under the mango tree or out of a garage, but in a huge facility with tall ceilings and an open floor plan on land that we actually owned. That once-shaky business model had been recognized by *Bloomberg Businessweek* as an innovative example of social entrepreneurship. Those once-subpar sandals, along with our line of beautiful accessories and apparel, had been featured in magazines like *Vogue* and spotted on national television and on A-list celebs.

We looked around and saw so many things that were once crazy pipe dreams *actually happening.*

But with that success came a lot of responsibility. We had employees in three countries and two continents. We had health insurance premiums to cover and 401(k)s to contribute to. We had a board of advisors that we reported to and investors to consider. We were selling a lot more stuff and making a lot more money, but we were spending a lot more too. Our bills were much higher and being off in our projections, even just a little bit, had much larger consequences than it once did.

Ben and I had graduated from living out of our car and were hoping to eventually transition out of our 300-square-foot apartment where we pirated internet from the restaurant next door. We had been trying to get pregnant for almost a year, suffering a miscarriage in the process and starting to wonder if this dream of building a family would be much more difficult (and potentially much more expensive) than we ever imagined. We were evolving both as a family and as a business, and all across the board, the stakes had certainly gotten much higher than they were in the early days.

During this season, while away for a weekend at a gathering with other entrepreneurs, Ben and I took advantage of the rare space away from the everyday grind and created the space for a Magic Wand meeting of epic proportions. We both had a feeling deep in ourselves that our business (and lives) could be even better. We just didn't really know how. As we entered into the sacred Magic Wand space, we promised one another we wouldn't talk about the HOW or what we've already tried or if we had the resources. We'd just wave our Magic Wand and lean in to say WOW.

If I had a magic wand . . .

Our business would create community and opportunity not just for women in East Africa, but here in the U.S. too.

Yes! And . . .

We'd be able to connect our customers to our makers in a way that was more meaningful, relational, and transformative.

Yes! And . . .

We'd somehow be able to tap into the creative, DIY, makers-movement and give all our customers access to their inner designers to create one-of-a-kind, custom goods.

Yes! And . . .

We'd never have to deal with a huge retailer and their un-reasonable terms and conditions again.

Yes! And . . .

We'd be a social enterprise that helped democratize impact entrepreneurship and teach other people how to start and run and grow their own businesses with a positive impact.

Yes! And . . .

We'd be profitable and actually get to pay ourselves consis-tently and raise a family together, ideally not in a 300 square-foot-apartment.

Those were some really big Magic Wand footprints to fill. But every single one of them left us with a sense of excitement and, well, *WOW*. Up in a cabin in the Catskills of New York, a million miles away from our employees and bills and the pres-sure to just keep our heads down, oh boy did we WOW. Our WOWing continued late into the night, where we sat around a campfire with other entrepreneurs we trusted to Yes, And! our dreams and the WOW just got louder and louder until it wove its way into our hearts for good. Buyers beware: once you really WOW, it's hard to go back to status quo.

In the following weeks and months of HOWing our WOW, we realized that very few of these dreams were possible within the existing framework of the business we had spent seven years of blood, sweat, and tears (so many tears) building. We had over 600 stores that were carrying our products, and we had lived out of our car and pounded the pavement (literally) to win many of those accounts. We had employees and sales reps and systems and technology and financing in place to support a business model that couldn't support most of these dreams.

But oh my gosh, by the end of that Magic Wand meeting, the energy of WOW was *palpable*.

When we made our way back to Portland and started in on the HOW PLAN, we came up with an idea of how we could actually achieve these goals. When we told our board we wanted to shut down the retail channel that accounted for over 75 percent of revenue, they (rightfully) thought we were off our rockers. So did our employees. And our banker. And my hair stylist.

But by this point, we were intoxicated by WOW.

Within the next year, we ended up running a few top-secret pilot tests and put our product and story into the hands of some of our most enthusiastic customers who wanted to become more a part of the Sseko Story, style their friends, and earn an income. There was Gena, the seamstress from Coal Country and Monique, the homeschooling mama in Texas. Anna, the brilliant and kind graduate student from Portland. Danielle, the hilarious farmer's wife from Indiana. The free-spirited grandmother named Hope and Alyssa, the ambitious, aspiring impact entrepreneur from Missouri. There was Christina, who was a doula from Washington and Caroline, a salty paralegal from New York City. They had different backgrounds and experiences and skills, but what they did have in common was a deep belief that all women are worthy of a sisterhood who will stand with them and the mischievous inkling that perhaps they could be a part of a story bigger and more adventurous than they ever imagined. (And a soft spot for building a wardrobe full of beautiful handbags, footwear, and apparel. One cannot deny the unifying force of the love of the *perfect* purse.) We called them The Sseko Fellows. Though we were shaking in our boots, we put out the call and they applied to become the pioneers of the sisterhood that is still growing to this day. Within several months of launching this rinky-dink pilot program, our top Fellows were outselling our top retailers. Returns and exchanges were down and customer satisfaction was up.

The Sseko Fellows started connecting with one another in ways that we couldn't have imagined. As their businesses started to grow, so did they: in confidence and curiosity and courage and passion and friendship. Instead of going to massive tradeshows in Vegas where we breathed recycled convention air and suffered from fluorescent lighting fatigue, we hosted our first retreat for our Fellows on the Oregon coast, where by day we taught Sseko Fellows from all around the country how to run and grow their businesses and connected with one another around a campfire at night. We saw as women started stepping out of loneliness and isolation and into purpose and community. Instead of paying for tradeshow booths and retail displays, we started spending money on increasing compensation for our Fellows, and in turn, they started earning more, quitting their full-time jobs and supporting their families with their Sseko business. Instead of spending money on online advertising, we started putting those dollars aside, so we could take Fellows to Uganda to meet their colleagues and have the adventure of a lifetime and have their worlds crack open in the way mine had been cracked open so many years before. Instead of begging retailers to answer our emails and pay their bills on time, we started investing that time and money in building a system that would allow our customers to design their own products from start to finish and connect with the maker with radical relationality like never before.

We decided that connection was the currency we wanted to deal in, and we went *all in.*

It some ways, we were starting from scratch. Nearly seven years in, we found ourselves *back* on the road doing trunk shows and hosting events in order to find new Sseko Fellows. We found ourselves *yet again* sleeping on pull-out couches, this time with a chubby miracle baby in tow.

Within a (grueling and very sleep-deprived) year, we had *tripled* our revenue *and* our impact.

But perhaps what is most exciting to me is that I can say, nearly ten years into running this company, I've never felt more *on purpose* in my work than I do today. In addition to creating dignified jobs and opportunities for wicked-smart girls in East Africa, I get to lead entrepreneurs here in the U.S. as they build their own lives and stories of impact, purpose, and passion. I get to walk alongside women who have courageously decided to wake up, show up, and be on assignment in their own lives.

And it all started with a Magic Wand session and some serious WOWs.

Pluckies, whether you're just starting out or you're decades into building the business, family, community, or life of your dreams, you've got to give that little idea or dream or vision just a few seconds to emerge into the world and take a big gasp of air before you sign it up for American Ninja Warrior HOW Challenge. Let yourself get just a little tipsy on the WOW before you get out the whiteboard and start in with HOW. Don't worry, most of the dumb ideas will not survive the gauntlet of HOW but sometimes the very best ideas just need a little extra time in the hands of wonder to grow their little wings and begin to take flight.

So next time the whisper of a dream, no matter how Big or Small, enters your imagination, may I *implore you*: before hacking that innocent dream to death with a HOW Hatchet . . .

STOP.

DROP.

And WOW.

INTERLUDE

Gulu, Uganda > London, England > **Portland, Oregon**

After plenty of WOWing there will, of course, come a time to get serious about the HOW. The good news is, there is very little in the world that you cannot figure out *how* to do once you're fueled by a jetpack full of WOW. In the journey of building a life of passion and purpose, the vast majority of steps just aren't rocket science. We have more resources than ever at our fingertips and you'd be amazed at what YouTube, a pile of books, and some podcasts can help you figure out.

Gather up the pluck to ask someone who's an expert in what you need to learn, and you'd be shocked at the number of people who will say yes to an invitation for coffee and an informational interview. There are piles and piles of pure gold in these meetings.*

---

*As someone who is often now on the other side of these meetings, please do not ask for a meeting with someone so you can "pick their brain." First off, if you really stop to think about it, this is a weird and ambiguous phrase. Instead, explain who you are, why you want to meet with them, a few specific questions, and what you

But, speaking from experience, you do incur some risk when you start to surround yourself with people who are smarter and more accomplished than you. While it is necessary, and 100 percent worth said risk, don't say I didn't warn you; you are consenting to the possibility of utter and complete mortification. That's okay. It's just part of the deal.

In the early days of our business, a few months into our cross-country road trip, we were sleeping in someone's basement in Portland. Through a friend of their friend, I was able to score a lunch meeting with a top-level executive at a footwear company that will remain nameless but that every single one of you would recognize. I was *so nervous*. I was so very ignorant and new to our industry that I truly didn't know if I'd be able to even hold a conversation. He was in the later stages of his career, a 30-year veteran in the footwear and manufacturing biz.

So, Tuesday rolls around and here I am in this nice restaurant with this 50-ish-something-year-old man who was generous enough to spend an hour with me. We were about halfway through lunch and while I was by no means *thriving*, I was surviving. I was taking furious notes and learning a ton. The conversation turned to supply chain and he was asking me something about the cost of one of our raw materials and luckily for me, I had just done a little bit of research comparing what our cost of goods was in East Africa compared to China, where his company did all their manufacturing. My "research" had simply consisted of hopping online and going to Alibaba.com. (If you're not familiar, Alibaba is one of the largest websites in the world. It's like Amazon but for Chinese factories.)

---

hope to accomplish in the meeting. People do not generally want to take time out of their busy days to shoot the breeze and have their brain picked, ew, by a random stranger. But they are usually more than willing to meet with someone who has at least a few specific questions to ask or objectives in mind.

I was actually feeling quite good that I had an informed answer for his supply chain question when he asked me, "Where did get that information?"

You know when you're reading a book and you come across a name that you don't quite know how to pronounce so you just make something up? (Like Hermione in Harry Potter? I said Herm-e-own until I saw the movie.) You're just minding your business reading your book and you have ZERO intentions of ever saying the character's name out loud, so you kinda just go with the first thing that pops in your head.

Well, I did that with Alibaba.com. For all I cared at the time, it was just a random Chinese website that I had no intention of talking about out loud.

So, when this very important executive asked me where I found this information, without mentally processing it one iota before I confidently answered him, I said out loud what I had been saying in my head all along: A Labia Dot Com.

A
Labia
Dot
Com

A
LABIA
Dot
Com

Perhaps what's worse is that even once I had so confidently and inappropriately used the word LABIA, it *still* didn't click with me. I was so used to saying it that way in my head that even once it left my mouth, it just felt right. So, naturally, as one does after they answer a simple question with a simple statement I just politely stared at him and waited for him to respond.

He looked at me wide-eyed and somewhat befuddled that in addition to casually saying LABIA at the lunch table, I didn't seem at all fazed by it. Ball's in your court, bud. (No pun intended.*)

After a period of uncomfortable and confusing silence, he looked at me and said *deadpan*: "Well, I try to stay off websites like that at work." He paused briefly as if he expected me to get the joke so we could finally move forward off this Island of Awkward together.

He threw me a *freaking lifesaver* as I was drowning, and I just looked at him completely dead in the eyes. I was confused by his statement and desperately trying to understand why he wouldn't be able to use a materials sourcing website at work when he finally just put me out of my misery and moved on to something else.

It was probably a full 30 seconds that went by before I put the pieces together, but IT WAS TOO LATE, YOU GUYS. What little tiny sliver of a window I had to salvage the situation was slammed shut. I couldn't go back. I couldn't explain myself. I couldn't make a joke and laugh at my mistake. After I put the pieces together and realized what had happened, I had to sit there, trying to listen to what he was talking about now as my face grew beet red, my heart started to race, and I grew pit stains the size of Lake Michigan.

I wanted to die. As he had moved onto the next topic, I casually looked down at what bits of chicken were left on my plate and I wished to God in Heaven that I was as dead as those strips of chicken and that a waitress would mercifully come by and whisk me away and dump me into the trash where I belonged.

I did not recover.

*Yes, yes of course it was.

The rest of the meeting was a blur and I ended up having to throw my shirt away because no amount of Tide could rid that shirt of the stench of my humiliation. Here was my first legitimate and important connection in the industry and I had gone and ruined it for both of us with unknowingly talking about genitalia over our Caesar Salads.

The moral of the story is: THIS COULD (AND PROBABLY WILL) HAPPEN TO YOU.

I stretched. I put myself out there and asked for the meeting with the person who was 100x more connected and resourced and knowledgeable than me and I made an absolute and total fool of myself.

But guess what? Although I fell asleep that night in a state of utter self-loathing humiliation, I'm still here. And that tiny, pie-in-the-sky business I was seeking guidance about? It's still here too. And both that company and I are a bit bruised and scraped up but we're bigger and stronger and more focused than ever.

Here is something you need to know: as you build a life of purpose and passion, your entire dream will feel like it's coming crashing down around you a thousand times.

And then?

The sun will rise.

Every time.

If you're not utterly humiliating yourself on a semi-regular basis, you're not stretching enough, Pluckie.

Keep stretching.

Keep learning and seeking guidance and surrounding yourself with people smarter than you and you will figure out how to execute your dreams. I'm not saying you won't make a fool of yourself in the process (in fact, I'm all but promising that you will) but if you're curious and open and pursue the vast amount of resources that are available to everyone with an internet connection and half a brain, it's entirely possible.

But remember not to diminish or deny the Power of Wow, even while you are waist deep in HOW. Like a granny who lived through The Great Depression saves her aluminum foil scraps, you've got to scrimp and save every ounce of WOW you come across. You've got to constantly be making deposits into The Bank of Wow because as long as you're growing and challenging yourself, you'll never stop accidentally saying "labia" at the exact wrong time. (Metaphorically speaking, of course.*)

*Hopefully.

TWELVE

Dream to Attract Your Team

For the first year of our marriage, we installed a whiteboard in our dining room and turned our closets and bathroom into inventory storage. The early days of our marriage involved listening to a lot of *This American Life* while we packed and shipped sandals and dreamed about the future when maybe our fulfillment center wouldn't be located in our living room.

We lived in an apartment in Kansas City, Missouri, that probably should have been condemned, but we loved it because it cost $395/month and was within walking distance of the local Irish pub. We lived next door to a guy named Thomas who we really connected with because he was also a side hustler! Gotta love a fellow hustler! Only we eventually learned that while we were hustling sandals, Thomas was hustling drugs. Thomas eventually moved to a nicer apartment while we downgraded to living out of our car, which leads me to believe that drugs have a better profit margin than fair-trade sandals; but that's neither here nor there. Sseko was not even close to being in a place where I could take a salary, so for that first year of marriage, we were both living off Ben's (very entry-level) income. What little we had left over, we'd pour back into the business. When times would get tough, I'd troll Craigslist to see what side gigs I could pick up to help supplement our sparse income.

Some people start with the dignified, full-time job and slowly grow their side hustle into full time. I decided to start full-time with The Dream and then side hustle my way to survival. Here's the thing about being really sold out on your dream: you lose every shred of pride. In the best way! Although I never did anything that went against my moral code, I cannot say I'd be *particularly proud* to show you the list of Side Hustle gigs I did during those early years just to scrape by.

* * *

During a particularly desperate season, I answered a Craigslist ad from a "Film Company" looking for a female between the ages of 20 and 30 who could do a "Northern European" accent and was available on weekends to film a "PG sci-fi comedy." Pay was $100/day. I wasn't sure if I could actually do any of those accents *well*, but surely for a hundred bucks I could pull off something that was vaguely believable! I met with "The Producers" (IN A PUBLIC PLACE YOU GUYS, IT'S FINE; TAKE A DEEP BREATH AND STOP WATCHING SO MANY LIAM NEESON MOVIES.) and learned that these two brothers were filming a *very* low-budget "sci-fi comedy." They had roped in enough of their friends to get the "cast" in place but they were still looking for someone who could play their long-lost sister who happened to be a warrior princess with an ambiguous European accent and magic warrior princess powers. They were nice (and nerdy) enough and I figured it would be a one- or two-day gig and we really needed the money, so I took the "job."

Turns out, this little "film gig" lasted almost a year. I was confused and kind of embarrassed by what I had gotten myself into, but mama's gotta help pay the bills and my "full-time sandal gig" certainly wasn't bringing home the bacon. Every dime we had was going right into investing in materials and paying Mary, Mercy, and Rebecca for their work. We tried more conventional ways of financing our business with a loan but got laughed out of every bank in town. (I think we met with and were rejected by about 13 banks over the course of two weeks. That was *rough*.)

But cash is king. And we needed it. So, for almost a year, while I am trying to take myself seriously as an entrepreneur, I would disappear for an entire Saturday and drive to the middle of nowhere Kansas where I'd film a chase scene in a wooded labyrinth, running after a ten-year old wearing a Chewbacca costume, wielding my plastic golden sword. It was all very glamourous and dignified and in line with my life plan.

False.

More like I'd cry myself to sleep at night with my college degree tucked under my pillow and wonder what I was doing with my life.

The "directors" would give me whatever wadded up chunk of cash they had on hand at the end of the day and I'd use it to buy groceries and then go back to my real life and pretend I'd been doing something that normal, cool, 24-year-olds who have their acts together do on Saturdays, like strolling the farmers market or brunching. Ben was obviously in on the secret but for the longest time, none of my friends would inquire when I'd show up late to weekend hangouts. Until the day when I walked into a restaurant to meet some gal pals for dinner and had forgotten to take my Magical Golden Sword out of my leather riding boots. I am pretty good at talking my way out of things, but explaining why I had a spray-painted plastic sword hidden in my boots for girl's night out was tricky. The inquisition quickly spiraled and the gig was up. I had been found out. While my friends were getting promotions and contributing to their 401(k)s I was doing, quite literally, anything for a buck to keep this little dream alive.

Here's the thing about chasing your dreams that not enough people will tell you: it's actually not at all about doing what you want when you want to and loving every minute of it. It's about doing the crappy things now that what will enable you to do want you want to do *most* tomorrow. And sometimes, to do what you want *most* tomorrow, it means sucking it up and chasing a tiny Chewbacca through the woods *today*.

✳ ✳ ✳

After the gig was up, I completely broke down and confided in my friend Molly that I was so stressed out that I couldn't sleep at night and was actually losing clumps of hair because, despite my endless side hustles and babysitting and weekend Warrior-Princessing, we couldn't afford to make payroll. Now, Molly had recently gotten her Certified Public Accounting degree and landed a job at a Big Four Consulting Firm. She had a steady paycheck, insurance, and retirement plan. Basically, she was everything my father wanted me to be. Sitting across the table from someone on such a steady and sure path, I felt ashamed and discouraged. But you know what happened after I stopped pretending to have it all together and let her see a peek behind the curtain? Molly listened. And then she proposed that she'd give a portion of her enviably steady income to help us bridge the gap for a few months. She believed so deeply in the work that we were doing, and she wanted to be a part of the story. Molly didn't know how to make sandals or have any desire to start a social enterprise. So instead, she gave out of what *she* had to offer: cold, hard cash. Which, turns out, is *exactly* what we needed in that moment. She stepped in. She bridged the gap. She's one of my very best friends to this day.

While mortifying in the moment, getting found out as moonlighting in a crappy sci-fi film on the weekends taught me a really powerful lesson: your dream will attract your team.

The good: your dream attracts your team. YAY! This is SO FUN.

The bad: mind-reading is not a skill most of us possess and your family, friends, and unsuspecting strangers are likely not sitting around, pontificating about how they can support you in your dreams they don't know about. You're going to have to put your big kid pants on, use your words, and *ask for help.*

The ugly: asking for help is one of the most vulnerable and courageous things you will ever do. And I all but promise that when you put your tender and hopeful heart out into the world, you will face rejection. Time and time again. More often than not, actually. You will be met with criticism, or perhaps worse, silence. Or *even worse*, a Bless-Your-Heart pity response. And this will sting, Pluckie. It *will* happen and it's gonna hurt *real bad.*

But I *promise you* the hurt is worth having a dream that eventually attracts your team. This is the good stuff. *Please* don't miss it. If you live your life trying to distance yourself from failure and protect yourself from rejection, you're going to also distance yourself from the life you are created to live, the impact you are made to make, and the unspeakably precious bonds you will create with those who join you.

* * *

Back in Uganda, we were finally able to afford our first machine. It was a *huge* milestone for us that was going to allow us to streamline our production and dramatically increase our consistency and quality. It was more money than we'd ever spent on anything and getting it to Uganda was no joke. We actually flipped a tiny, tin can pickup truck driving over massive potholes trying to get the machine to our workshop. When we finally got it to the workshop, the entire team was ecstatic. We showed the women how it worked and explained that whoever learned how to work the machine would receive a promotion and raise. When we asked who wanted to apply for the new job, there were *crickets*. What we didn't know is that some Ugandans consider working on machines to be "men's work" and not a single woman on our team wanted to risk the social cost of being a woman doing "men's work." Our hearts sank. We panicked. Here we had invested so much money and time into getting this machine and we did *not* see this coming. We could not afford to have this machine sit unused.

The next day we came back to the workshop and gathered the entire team around. We pitched our collective vision for how we wanted to see Sseko grow and the impact we could make for women in East Africa and across the globe. We painted a picture for how much better our product would be and how many women we could eventually employ and how many university scholarships we could eventually provide. But we explained that if we wanted to make a big impact, we needed to get *serious* about running a great business and best-in-class manufacturing facility. In a final desperate plea, we explained that we *needed* at least two women to step up to the plate and take on the challenge. We had dreamed big and now we were asking for someone to fill the gap.

After a terribly awkward silence, Joyce and Allen, two of the younger women on our team who came from particularly challenging backgrounds, felt especially compelled toward the idea of creating more jobs for other young women in their previous circumstances. They looked at one another, nodded their heads, and courageously both raised their hands. From that day on, Joyce and Allen became our beloved Machine Gals. Since we actually had no idea how to properly use the machine, we arranged for them to go to a factory across town that had a similar machine for a few days of training. When they walked into the machine area of the factory, the room full of men erupted in laughter. Joyce and Allen were openly mocked and jeered for being there to learn "men's work."

But nevertheless, they persisted.

Within just two days, Joyce and Allen got so good on the machine that a few months later, the owner of that factory came to *us* and asked if Joyce and Allen could help train some of their newest workers. Joyce and Allen proudly walked back into that factory in matching Machine Gal jumpsuits to *teach the men* how to do their jobs better, and those two became the stuff of *absolute legend* around these parts. We asked. They stepped in and bridged the gap.

* * *

Meanwhile in the U.S., we cast off what felt like the last cord tethering us to a safety net when Ben quit his full-time job, which was our only source of income, to join Sseko full-time. In the humid heat of a Kansas City summer, we spent days cooped up in our little apartment making a little stop-motion video explaining our plans for a nationwide tour to launch the brand. We had this huge dream that Sprint, based in Kansas City, would sponsor the tour. We'd be a living, breathing example of how you could run a company off their mobile internet and in turn they'd hook us up with a slick Airstream and free internet and it was going to be fancy and awesome and the stuff Millennial dreams are made of. We sent out the pitch we'd spent weeks and weeks creating. And then we followed up. And followed up again. And again. Crickets. Nothing. Nada. Not even the dignity of a rejection.

So instead, we sold everything we owned to finance the tour ourselves and lived out of our car, traveling the country in an effort to try and get this little fledgling dream to take flight. For six months, we lived out of our Honda Element and relied on the hospitality of complete strangers to join us in the journey by hosting trunk shows in their living rooms. We'd share the Sseko story and showcase our wares to these strangers like a couple of homeless sandal peddlers. And then? After opening their homes and introducing us to their friends, they'd often let us sleep on their couches and drink their coffee the next morning before we went back on the road, usually not knowing if that night we'd find ourselves sleeping in our car in a McDonald's parking lot or benefiting again from the sheer grace and generosity of strangers and their couches along the way. We cast the vision and then made the ask. And people stepped in. *Hundreds* of them. They bridged the gap. And now a few of these once-strangers are some of our closest friends. (We even got our first goddaughter out of the gig!*)

I get it. Being on the "needy" side of the equation never feels good *in the moment*. In fact, it usually feels *terrible*. When we live in fear, we hold back from pursuing our dreams and becoming who we were created to be because we are desperately afraid of facing rejection. We spend all our time dodging "No" instead of chasing after "Yes!" We miss out completely on the thrill and joy of standing on one side of the canyon and working alongside others to bridge the gap.

If you think it's even remotely possible that you build a life of purpose and passion without showing your humanity, facing rejection, and asking for help along the way, your gap is much too small. If building an international business and community has taught me anything, it's that The American Gospel of Self Reliance teaches us that the Gold Standard is achieving a life that keeps you from ever being in need. Just amass more! More money, more security, more walls, more insurance policies, more distance from your neighbors, more privacy, more, more, more.

So, we never let those small dreams turn into bigger, more audacious ones because we're terrified of The Gap. We're horrified about the prospect of being a burden, or of looking needy, or putting someone out. We live a muted and diluted life because we're too afraid of facing rejection. We never really say a big, terrifying, delicious YES because we are too afraid of the tiny nos that will inevitably come our way.

But, Pluckies, if your dream goes beyond achieving individual success and is actually something that will create a rising

*We love you, Addy Joy!!

tide not just for you but for those around you, that dream will eventually attract your team.

I define a visionary as someone who sees the gap between the way things are and the way they could be. And if you are really dreaming big, that "gap" is going to be more like a canyon. And that canyon cannot be bridged with a single bridge builder who is horrified at the idea of asking for help every once in a while.

When you vision the gap and then ask for help in building the bridge, you risk the awkwardness and embarrassment that comes from the inevitable "Nos." (There will be plenty of them.) But these momentary disappointments do not come *even close* to outweighing the brilliant joy and gratitude and magic that happens when someone finally does raise their hand and says, "Yes! I will bring my tools and I will build alongside you." Some will bring their pickup trucks and heavy machinery. Others will bring only a single nail and a hammer and stay for just a moment. But all of it is *pure magic*. There is nothing more humbling and awe-inducing and life-giving than standing alongside others, shoulder to shoulder, building something together that didn't exist before.

❊ ❊ ❊

It's that time in the book where I share a little science with you. And this science is going to blow. yo. mind. We're afraid to stretch so far and dream so big that we might need a little help along the way. Why? Because we want people to like us. We all love to be loved. It's part of the being-a-human gig.

SO, you think every time you ask for a favor or need help it's going to make people like you a little less, don't you? It's common sense, right? Every time you ask for help you're making a withdrawal from your likeability bank. *Asking* for help makes people like us less and *giving* help makes people like us more, right?

Wrong.

Check this: it's called the Benjamin Franklin effect.[1] According to good ole Benjy himself, "He that has once done you a kindness will be more ready to do you another, than he whom you yourself have obliged." Simply put, someone who does you a favor will feel *more* fondly toward you and therefore be *more likely* to help you out in the future.

Here is how the legend goes: there was a man of "fortune and influence" who disliked Benjamin Franklin. But Benjy knew he'd need him on his side eventually, so he plotted how to win his favor. Counterintuitively, instead of doing something nice for this guy, Benjy asked the man if he could borrow a treasured book from his personal library. The man obliged and Benjy returned the book a week later with a thank-you note. The next time they saw one another, the man was decidedly *more* friendly toward him. And get this: they then forged a genuine friendship that lasted for the rest of their lives.

But don't just take Benny Boo Bear's word for it. What do the modern-day scientists have to say about this little theory?

In a study done at the University of Texas,[2] scientists had participants in three separate groups engage in an intellectual contest where students could win a significant sum of money. After the students were given their winnings, the following happened:

- Group One: The person who performed the study told the students that he was passionate about the research but had been using his own funds and was running out of money. He asked the students if they'd return the money to him, so he could keep running the study.

- Group Two: The students were approached by a secretary and told that the psychology department was running low on funds and she asked the students if they would return the money to the department.
- Group Three: The students were not approached and left with their winnings.

Then all three were surveyed to see how much they liked the researcher.

Group Two rated him lower than Group Three which indicates that an *impersonal* request for a help *decreases* liking.

But Group One rated him *higher* than Group Three (!!!) which indicates that *a personal request* for a favor increases affection, even more than having never asked at all!

The science behind this psychological phenomenon is called *cognitive dissonance*. Our brains clump things together because these "pairings" and "general rules" help us process information as quickly and efficiently as possible.

Here is one of these rules: when we like someone, we want to help them. They go together in our brains: affection and favors.

So, when we help someone out, whether we like them or not, it makes us *feel like we like them more* because, peanut butter and jelly. They go together. Affection and favors.

In another study done at Hosei University in Japan,[3] both Japanese and American participants who were asked for help by another participant reported increased levels of not only affection but also perceived closeness of the relationship.

It's not an accident that those who have gotten me out of a Giant Pickle or two have often gone on to become My People. Affection and favors go together. Showing our humanity to one another increases intimacy and connection.

And when you are the one who is brave and bold enough to *ask first*, you know what happens? You give permission for others to ask too.

That's not a burden, Pluckie. That's an *absolute gift*.

It's one thing to say, "Call me if you need anything!" Guess how many people will take you up on that offer ever? No one. It's stupid fluff that we all hear but don't really believe. When is the last time you casually said that to someone and they actually called you up out of the blue? Probably never. This is the reason we can be surrounded by people who seem nice enough, but truly lonely in our journeys.

When you have the courage to show your humanity and ask for help first, you're tugging at a little thread in the invisible barrier of Pride and Self Reliance. And as you start to tug, it will slowly unravel the entire velvet curtain charade. By pulling at the thread you will create a path into a new universe of community and togetherness.

When you say yes to a new leadership position and you find yourself in over your head and needing to be in two places at once and you call a fellow parent at your kid's school to ask if they can do you a major solid and pick your kid up for you, you're pulling at the thread. When an opportunity arises for them, they'll say yes to the thing that makes their heart beat faster, even though they feel scared, because they'll know it's okay to ask for help. *You* gave them that permission.

When you're trying to build a beautiful family but you're at the breaking point and instead of living in a house of shame, pretending your marriage is perfect and thriving, you call up another couple and you say, "We need help. Can we come over to talk something through? We need to bring some things into the light." You're pulling at the thread, brave one. When the time comes, they will know it's okay to come out of hiding and ask for help too. By going first, *you* taught them that.

When you commit to helping a woman who is in an abusive relationship find a safe place for her and her kids, even though you've got a sink full of dirty dishes and an impending work deadline, and you reach out to your book club to ask for leads on an apartment and help covering her first month of rent, you're pulling at the thread. When the time comes and *they* come across a need, they'll commit to bridging the gap, because they know they won't have to figure it out alone. They'll know they can call on others to help step in to build the bridge. By saying yes before you had a plan and by asking for help, you set the example. You paved the way for them to do the same.

We *love* being the one who gets to help. Being a helper is safe and it feels good to be needed. But when you finally take off the one-dimensional Helper costume you've so carefully crafted over the years and let yourself grow into the Giver/Receiver that you really are, this act of bold truthfulness will be a light.

It may not feel like it in the moment, but make no mistake: you're not just asking for help. You're also giving a sacred gift: permission for others to do the same. You are courageously, thread by thread, dismantling the crippling shroud of shame that teaches us to be embarrassed of our needs. You're creating an opening to a new reality of community and interdependence and shame resilience.[4] Asking for help is really saying,

"Don't be afraid to dream big too. You're not alone. Let's do this together."

So, dream the dreams and live the life that will surely have you asking for help every once in a while. Say yes before you've got it all figured out. Allow your curiosity to take you to an unknown place where there is a chasm that you *have no earthly idea* how you're going to bridge. Don't just Mind the Gap but *create* it. Then ask for help in building the bridge and watch as your dream attracts your team.

And the next time you're standing in the gap and someone inevitably raises their brow and says, "Excuse me, your humanity is showing," you just smile mischievously and say, "I know."

THIRTEEN

Don't Hide from The Shadows

In the second grade, we read *The Lion, the Witch and the Wardrobe* by C. S. Lewis. I'd go home at night and my mom and I would reread the chapter I had just heard hours before at school. I devoured every word. Shortly after we finished the book as a class, I showed up at school one day and our teacher told us that we'd be watching the movie version and I panicked.

And then I *refused*.

In what was perhaps my first attempt at conscientious objection, I asked Ms. Stout for special permission to sit out in the hallway while the rest of the class watched the movie.

I refused to watch because I was *terrified* that my picture of this mystical world of Narnia and these characters who had become dear friends would be shattered if I saw someone else's vision of them. I didn't believe that my imagination was strong enough to hold fast and pure onto *my* picture of Narnia, of Lucy and Mr. Beaver, if I watched someone else's version of them on a glowing screen.

I'm not quite so sure why protecting my version of Narnia felt so imperative, but looking back, I think it's because my first and most formative picture of God was learned through Mr. Lewis's make-believe world and his depiction of The Divine, who in the story, took the form of a lion named Aslan.

> "Aslan is a lion—the Lion, the great Lion," said Mr. Beaver.
> "Ooh," said Susan. "I'd thought he was a man. Is he quite safe? I shall feel rather nervous about meeting a lion. . . ."
> "Safe?" said Mr. Beaver. "Who said anything about safe? 'Course he isn't safe. But he's good. He's the King, I tell you."[1]

Decades later, I whisper Lewis's prose about a lion named Aslan to my sons each night before I lay them down to sleep. *He isn't safe. But he's good.*

The journey to building your purpose, the reason for which you were created is *not safe, but it is good.*

C. S. Lewis also says, "There is no safe investment. To love at all is vulnerable. Love anything, and your heart will certainly be wrung and possibly broken."[2]

Travelers, this wisdom applies to our purpose and passion too. I need you to hear me say that this journey is beautiful and life giving. But that does not mean it is easy or free of heartache. When did we start selling and buying the line that "Finding Our Passion" is synonymous with happy and light? If the path you're on and those who are leading you are promising that it will only be bright and shiny and happy, I'm going to ask you to be suspicious.

It is not safe, *but it is good.*

I meet hundreds or maybe thousands of people a year, and often hear remarks about how joyful and optimistic I am, dreaming these Big Dreams and inviting others to join me on the winsome adventure of life. And while the depth of my joy and fulfillment is real, this is not the whole story. Because in addition to having bold and beautiful dreams, I also have nightmares.

I'm not being metaphorical here. I'm talking about good old-fashioned, middle-of-the-night, cry-out-in-your-sleep nightmares.

Not of boogeymen or dark figures chasing me, but cinematic pictures of the horrors that I have come to learn through this journey face women all over the world—here and there. Occasionally, the stories of heartache and violence and loneliness and injustice and stigma and oppression that have been entrusted to me over the past decade find their way into my dreams.

The first time my husband, Ben, experienced this charming part of spending the night with me, I awoke from the nightmare and was lying beside him, sobbing. He thought I was still asleep and captive to the dream. He tenderly tried to wake me, holding me while whispering, "It's OK. You're asleep. It's just a nightmare. It's not real."

"But I *am* awake," I cried. "And it *is* real. Not for me, but for her." And I wept until sunrise.

Because when you decide to use your life and your gifts and your privilege to make the world a little brighter and more just and fair, you're going to discover just how dark the darkest corners are. This, Travelers, is The Shadow Side of the work we were created to do.

In this cultural moment, we're *obsessed* with "passion," but like a bad game of telephone, the whole story has gotten twisted somewhere along the way. We say we want to be passionate, but then we build lives that keep us safe from that very thing.

Did you know that the root of the word *passion* is the Latin word *pati*, which means to suffer?

Suffer.

Take a moment and reflect on that word, *suffer*.

Distress

Misery

Trauma

Torment

Pain

Agony

Anguish

I must warn you that there are people going around these days promoting a dangerous idea. They are telling you that when you "Find Your Passion" you will finally be *happy*. We want to be happy, of course! Happy isn't bad. But it isn't the whole story. It's not the final destination. And if we believe it is, we will build lives that attempt to keep us from all the things that could possibly break our hearts. But in doing so, our lives become containers so shallow that they cannot hold much of anything at all.

True passion and purpose and joy cannot be contained in the shallow pools constructed only for easy and bright. Passion can only be contained in wells deep enough to also hold sorrow and grief. The degree to which you can experience true joy and lasting fulfillment is equal to the degree to which you hold space for darkness and questions.

We are made to believe that grief is a robber of joy and darkness a thief of the light. But the truth is, the world is a beautiful and horrible place. And when we build walls tall enough to keep out the Horrible, we become impenetrable to the Beauty too.

* * *

About two years into running our business, I received a call from a colleague. I can still hear, with haunting clarity, the sound of stifled cries on the other end of the line as the words were still forming.

I waited.

And the words finally came.

It wasn't a statistic or a carefully crafted message about gender-based violence meant to pull at the heartstrings. It was the raw and messy middle of a story of violence and trauma against a woman who had become a dear friend, trusted colleague, and integral part of our work. This woman is casting a vision and lighting a path for the women who will come after her in a way I could never do. She is a force and she is a light.

The specifics of her trauma are not mine to tell.

But what I will tell you is that her story sent me careening into The Shadow Side in a way I had never experienced before. It left me breathless and heartbroken and grief-stricken, pleading to understand how and why such evil and darkness exists.

A million **whys**.

A cacophonous symphony of **whys**, beating mercilessly without an end.

As I listened to these words and her story, I fell deeper into the darkness and I cried out to God with desperation

please

please

please.

Please do not let this extinguish her Light. The world needs her Light. I couldn't pray for what was done to her to be un-done. But I could beg that *somehow*, her Light would survive The Dark.

Travelers, I refuse to encourage you to Dream Big and Make an Impact without warning you that that at some point in your pursuit, you might also find yourself with a broken heart, angry and afraid and making wild, nonsensical promises in exchange for mercy, in exchange for a miracle.

Hours, days, weeks after, I realized I was still falling.

My constant song became one of pleading, of begging. But there was only silence.

Slowly and stealthily, without my even knowing it, the empty space that the silence created started to fill in. It filled with burning anger toward those who enacted the violence and a world that permits it.

And then the questions without answers set in.

Was this random? An occupational hazard of being born a girl in this world? If so, how does one begin to grieve and chip away at this gruesome and unjust punishment for being female?

Or was this a calculated, *political act* intended to send a message about what happens to *girls like her* who dared to dream beyond the small part they were handed to play?

And if so, what does *that* mean?

Who the hell am *I* anyway, believing like a stupid, fool-ish child that perhaps me and my stupid ideas and idealistic wishes and foolish dreams could actually make a difference in a world *this* broken?

The joke is on me.

It will never get better. Not for women there. Not for women here. It's always been this way and it always will be. We're too far gone. The world is too broken and evil.

So, move on from your little "equality and justice crusade."

Go back to Square One.

Because Square One is easy and it's bright and it's full of hope and questions that have easy answers. Square One is filled with simple taglines like "One for One" and "Change for a Dollar." On Square One, I am told I can "Change the World" without more effort or sacrifice than it takes to buy a latte! Square One is safe and shallow and cannot possibly contain this depth of pain and questioning, so, yes, I think I'll go back to Square One now.

No one told me that "Making an Impact" would mean anxiety attacks and grief and excusing myself during the middle of a team meeting to run down the hall to vomit as quietly as possible while crying out to God and hearing nothing in response but the echo of my own questions.

No one told me that good things are built not in hours or days or weeks. But in years, in decades, with joy *and* sorrow, with laughter *and* tears, with answers you will come to believe deep in your soul and questions that will ultimately demand your surrender.

And if we buy the line that "Finding Our Passion" and "Changing the World" brings *only* clean and bright happiness and self-satisfaction, we'll bounce from "cause" to "cause," changing our profile photos and purpose du jour, all the while making sure our hearts stay unscathed in the process, knowing that when

the darkness sets in

when the hard questions arise

when the complexity fogs our pristine and naive glasses
when grief comes knocking at our door
we can jump ship and let the waves of newness and
    adrenaline fill in the parts of us that were created not
    just to hold new and shiny and bright and exciting
    success but to hold space for The Shadows too.

After years and years of pleading to understand the degree of evil and violence and injustice that exists in our world, I still don't know why and probably never will. But perhaps even scarier is that if you continue in the work to become who you were created to be, the questions first directed at the evil Out There, will eventually beg to be asked in the quiet stillness of yourself.

In the last decade, I've been labelled a "Do-Gooder" and "World Changer" and I have to say, those labels that I once desperately strove for and found immense satisfaction in make me increasingly uncomfortable these days. Over the past ten years of doing the work that has earned me accolades and awards and applause, there is also the quieter, messy, terrifying, and never-ending work of turning the questions I once directed out at The World inward toward myself.

For each of us, the questions will vary, but if they feel scary and complex, it's a good sign they are the very questions you should be asking.

How do I both acknowledge and use my privilege in a way that truly creates a rising tide? How am I currently benefiting from centuries of racism and oppression and violence and what do I do with that? How much of the brokenness in the world that I am trying to help fix was caused by *my* ancestors in the first place and what does that mean? How do I acknowledge that my privilege and my blind spots and my naivete and my good intentions could actually hurt and demean those I want most to serve and uplift?

How do I acknowledge the complexity of it all without becoming utterly and completely paralyzed?

As you pursue your purpose and strive to make a positive impact in the world, you might be tempted to believe in a dangerous false dichotomy:

We can be people who build lives that will keep us from ever having to ask the hard questions and who will never leave Square One where it is bright and shiny and simple. With bricks made of our privilege and comfort and soothing self-satisfaction, we can build taller walls to protect us from The Shadows and the questions without easy answers.

or

We can succumb to the false belief that *all* the world's problems are ours to solve and become so overwhelmed with the enormity of brokenness—both in the world and in ourselves—that we wave the white flag. With bricks made of cynicism and resigned apathy, we eventually start building walls.

With either choice, brick by brick, we will build little fortresses around our hearts and lives to keep us safe and distanced from The Shadows that we know would break our hearts.

But perhaps we shouldn't be afraid of the Shadow Side and of our breaking hearts. Perhaps we should be more afraid of the bricks, of building that fortress that promises to keep us safe, stone by stone. Because what is more hopeful and haunting and human than a broken heart, filled with a million little cracks, spidering across, letting the Light shine in—and if we're lucky, maybe occasionally letting the Light shine out too?

No one else can go into The Shadow Side for you. We need *you* to go. When you decide to bear your torch and march into The Shadows, no matter how delicate and dim your flame, you're showing us that we can go too.

We were not made to be master escape artists who can move through life, avoiding The Shadows. We were created to make space for both the darkness and the light. For deep joy and deep sorrow. For questions that do not have an answer and for the deep, rooting truths that will keep us moving forward as we become part of The Whole.

We are not created to build taller walls but to dig deeper the well that holds both beauty and brokenness. Digging deeper the well is not easy or pleasant or safe. In fact, it can be very painful. But, make no mistake, you are digging the depths of *both* the joy and sorrow that your heart can contain. You don't get one without the other. As you put down your bricks and instead dig deeper the well, the dirt beneath your nails becomes a sign of the sacred work you were created to do.

It is not safe, but it is *good*.

FOURTEEN

Walk One Another Home

Several years back, I was busy building our company in Uganda and in the U.S. Through our work-study program in Uganda, we were providing scholarships and enabling some of the brightest women in the country to continue on to university. We had a thriving full-time team who were making the most beautiful products, but more importantly, who day by day were starting to believe that they deserved more than the narrative they were handed.

And as we met goals and our company continued to grow and thrive in Uganda, my curiosity got the best of me. I couldn't help but start to wonder and dream if what we were doing in Uganda could be done in Ethiopia too. I had no idea how I'd make that happen, but I couldn't shake the feeling. I wanted to learn. To explore. To see if there was any possibility.

So, I hopped on a plane. No plan. No connections. (Are you sensing a theme in my life?)

I showed up in a new country where I knew almost no one, didn't speak the language, and had no plan.

And you know what happened?

This time, within a day of arriving in Ethiopia by myself with no plan, I found myself in a terrible, scary, this-is-exactly-what-your-mama-warns-you-against situation.

Upon landing, I found a guest room that was basically an empty storefront that had been converted into a hostel on the fourth floor of a mini-mall. It was $9/night and in a convenient part of town. And there was a tire shop in the next room! I mean, what more could a gal want? (I am still waiting for my Hilton Honors points from that stay to post to my account.)

Once I got settled in my room, I ventured out to buy a SIM card for my phone only to realize that my cell phone was not compatible with the Ethiopian network. I had no access to internet and no telephone. My husband knew what country I was in, but not much more than that because I had no way of touching base with him.

No big deal. It was a Friday, and on Saturday I'd have the entire day to get my ducks in a row, buy a phone, and find some internet so I could get to work exploring and dreaming and building.

Only, I didn't quite make it to that productive Saturday morning.

A few hours after landing in Addis Ababa, I started feeling sick. By Friday afternoon, I was dizzy and nauseous enough that I had to head back to my mini-mall guest room and lie down. Just for a minute.

I woke up hours later. The sun had set. I was covered in sweat and shivering. And my body was so sore I could barely move.

No phone.

No internet.

No friends.

The only person I "knew" was the owner of the guest room, Baharu, who had an office down the hall from the hostel room.

The sun had already set, and I knew if Baharu wasn't already gone, he would be leaving soon for the weekend. And I knew that once he left, there would be no one to help me.

I needed to tell someone I wasn't well.

I needed help.

I managed to crawl out of my bed, out of the guest room, and down the tiled, florescent-lit, mini-mall hallway. The shops were all closed and locked up with steel gates and padlocks, but at the end of the hall, I saw the storefront he had converted into his office with the door halfway open. Praise be, he was still there. I knocked on the open door and without even greeting him just managed to eek out: "I'm not feeling so well, Baharu."

My voice was shaking with a mix of embarrassment, fear, and sheer exhaustion. This virtual stranger took one look at me and immediately stood up from his office chair.

"Oh my goodness. Oh my goodness. Miss Leeez. What is wrong?" He came around his desk and placed his hand on my forehead. "Oh my goodness. We're going to hospital. You're fevering very high. You're very ill."

He made a few calls on his cell phone, speaking rapidly in Amharic before hanging up his phone and ushering me out of his office.

He placed his arm under me, supporting me as we descended four stories of mini-mall stairs down to the parking lot, where he helped me into his car. He explained in broken English that we were going to a hospital just down the road where his friend was the doctor.

As I drifted in and out of consciousness, I tried to imagine where we were going. I had been in the country for less than 24 hours and certainly had no context for what an Ethiopian hospital might look like.

The car began to slow, and I took my aching head out of my hands and looked up. I saw a white, blocky, single-story cement building with a hand-painted red cross near the front door.

We pulled around the corner and parked on the street. Baharu told me to wait while he came around the car and helped me out. With his arm underneath mine, we walked toward the clinic.

I walked into a room with plastic chairs lining all four walls. Every chair was filled and there were dozens of people standing, milling, squatting. It was rainy season and the dirt mixed with the water that rain-soaked patients were tracking in left a yellow-tiled floor smeared in mud.

Everything in the clinic was written in Amharic. Every sign, every poster, every door label looked like hieroglyphics to me. Except, plastered all over the clinic were copies of white computer paper with black letters, curiously in English, that read:

Meningitis Outbreak Warning!!!!
Signs of meningitis:

High, sudden fever.
Sore neck.
Confusion.

My heart started racing and my fogginess was momentarily cleared with a burst of lucid panic fueled by adrenaline. My fever was raging and had come on in a matter of hours. I was fuzzy and on the brink of losing consciousness. And my entire body, neck included, was very sore.

Baharu walked over to me, leaned in, and said, "It's time," and gently guided me by my elbow down a short hallway into a smaller clinic room. I walked in and there was a man sitting in a chair just beside the entryway. He was moaning, rocking back and forth. Occasionally, his moans would be interrupted, as if by another person, with a sharp cry of pain. Tears of fear and exhaustion welled up in me. A technician drew my blood and then sent me back to the waiting room. A while later, the doctor called me back to his office and explained in broken English that I did not in fact have meningitis but that I did have a severe infection and needed "an injection" quickly. What he was able to communicate in English had me feeling uncomfortably confused, so I asked to see the test results, which was futile because I can't actually read blood test results even in English, let alone in Amharic.

The doctor insisted that I needed an injection immediately. That this was the only way to stop the raging fever before it did "permanent damage." It *obviously* went against some good sense to let an unfamiliar someone inject me with an unfamiliar medicine for an unfamiliar infection, but the words "permanent damage" were pretty compelling too. So, I consented.

They led me to yet another room, where there were two nurses. I rolled up the right sleeve of my sweater and emotionally prepared myself for another needle.

But before I even managed to roll my sleeve all the way up, a nurse walked over and rolled it back down. Confused, I looked at her and she pointed to a cold, steel gurney pushed up against the wall.

"Go to sleep," she said.

Go to sleep? Call me crazy, but I was not expecting a terse lullaby in this moment. As I was clearly a little taken aback and not abiding by her instructions, she placed her hand on my ponytail and led me, head first, to the bed, all the while saying, "You. Lady. Go to sleep. Sleep. You go to sleep."

And in that moment, I thought, well, that is exactly what might happen. Goodnight, world. See ya, life. Lights out. Bye, bye.

The next thing I know, that nurse has her hands poised on the waistband of my pants, underwear included, and she forcibly removes both pieces of clothing in one practiced de-pantsing swoop.

So now I am lying there, naked from the waist down, in front of two women who didn't even a little bit try to hide their laughter at seeing a VERY pale rear end that hasn't seen the sun since circa 1987. I was much too ill to care that I was, quite literally, the butt of the joke.

A moment later, Nurse #2 spun around with not one, but two full syringes and GIANT NEEDLES held in her fists, arms bent at 90-degree angles in front of her face.

Two needles, one butt cheek. No warning. She just made a slight grunting noise as she stabbed me with what felt like a giant, forked cattle prod. As she pushed the medicine through the needles and into my unsuspecting cheek, the entire lower half of my body seized up.

"Relax! Relax!" And as if the stabbing wasn't enough, she was now slapping my bare butt repeatedly saying, "Relax! Lady! Go to sleep!"

After "sleeping" on the metal gurney for what I think was another few hours, the nurses woke me and took me back out to the waiting room where I was instructed to, "No move."

I had never been so afraid and so very alone.

But there sitting in the waiting room, *hours* later by now, was Baharu. I had known him for less than 24 hours and yet, he waited for me. A day-old friend whose face provided a remarkable sense of comfort and familiarity.

He motioned to the chair next to him and I went and gingerly lowered myself into the seat beside him. Baharu would occasionally pat me on the back and tell me he was "so, so sorry." And that "Everything going to be OK."

And somehow, impossibly, I believed him. Everything *would* be okay.

More than okay, in fact.

Because my Worst-Case Scenario was actually *exactly* where I was supposed to be.

Sitting there in that waiting room, I realized that I hadn't come to Ethiopia to "help" to "solve" or to "build" anything. Ending up scary sick in a foreign clinic, alone, butt-naked on a metal gurney wasn't a detour.

It was the whole point.

After years of building something truly beautiful in Uganda, this experience was meant to be a profound reminder that although I happened to be in a season of creating and giving, visioning and executing, at the end of the day, as Ram Dass says, "We're all just walking each other home."[1]

Sometimes we are in seasons of giving. Others in times of receiving.

Usually some of both.

Always just walking one another home.

At this realization, I became so overwhelmed with gratitude that I started to cry.

Here *I* was the foreigner, the alien, the burden, the needy, the receiver. *I* was in the very position most of us, myself included, try so desperately to avoid.

And yet. Here was a stranger, a brother, sitting beside me, with nothing to gain, who took care of me.

Every hour or so, the nurses would come out of the waiting room to take my temperature and give me a new, cool, dampened washcloth that I held against my forehead. After a few hours, my fever broke and the threat of "permanent damage" subsided and they told me I could return "home." As we walked past the registration desk at the front of the clinic, I started digging into my bag for cash to pay the bill for my services.

Baharu waved his hand at me and simply said, "It's taken care of," and we continued walking out of the clinic into the dark, rainy night. I was too exhausted to argue.

By the time we made it back to the hostel, it was the early morning. He took me back up the four flights of stairs to the guest room and helped me get settled. An hour or so later, he came to check on me and brought me a plate of French fries from the café downstairs, explaining that he figured I'd want something "American" to make me feel more comfortable.

Grace upon grace in the form of a greasy pile of French fries at 7 AM.

When I left Ethiopia a few weeks later, I put some cash to pay for my clinic visit and medicine in an envelope along with a thank-you letter and slipped it under Baharu's office door.

During a layover in Rome on my way home, I checked my email and found one from him, checking up on me. Toward the end of the email he wrote, "Liz, I was sad when you left your money in order to settle your debts. I thought you are my good friend and so no need to bother to pay at all."

Here I was trying to settle the bill, make it right and get myself back up to "even" when all he wanted was to walk me home.

✻ ✻ ✻

Two years ago, I took the Sseko Fellows on our first-ever group trip to Uganda. Leading adventure trips like this is obviously a major work perk. But I am going to shoot straight with you: I was excited but also *terrified*. Partly because many of the American women in this group had never even left the United States before and I knew even just the ratio of "guides" to "travelers" could make for a disaster of epic proportions.

But my bigger, more hidden fear was that, despite what felt like preaching ad nauseam that this trip was not for the purpose of helping or saving anyone but to learn more about how our products are made and to connect with the women who made them and have the adventure of a lifetime in a stunningly lush and vibrant country, I feared *deeply* that the narrative of The American Helper and the African Beneficiary was just too engrained to be overcome with my clumsy words and pep talks.

For weeks before the trip, I'd lie awake at night entertaining my Worst-Case Scenario that I'd be inadvertently wrangling a group of American women who thought they were doing someone a favor just by showing up to "Africa" in the first place.

Sweet baby Jesus, take the wheel.

I was scared, but I went anyway. Because more than anything, I believe in the power of proximity. The power in seeing what was once separated by an ocean, be that literally or symbolically, up close and nose to nose. The power in realizing,

209

over coffee or tea or laughter or tears or silence, that in fact, we share so much more in common than we ever could have imagined. So, together we went.

On the first day of the trip, while introducing ourselves at the workshop, I asked both our Sseko Uganda employees and our Sseko Fellows to share about their journey with Sseko and how they found themselves sitting in this workshop in Uganda.

The first Sseko Fellow to speak also happened to be the very first woman who said yes to joining us in this adventure. Through a shaky voice, Gena shared deeply and vulnerably about where she was when she first discovered this scrappy little sandal company and decided to join us. She shared about how she'd been toiling away in a corporate job she hated, raising two kids on energy fumes and trying to keep her then-fragile marriage together in the midst of being worn thin. She had spent years and years trying so hard to play the part she thought she was supposed to play, and she got lost somewhere along the way.

She shared how this global sisterhood, slowly and not without the growing pains that accompany courage, had helped bring her back home to herself. About how the story of this collective ambition to create community and opportunity and beautiful things with beautiful stories reminded her of who she was and the role she plays in the Big Story. She shared how the stories of both her Ugandan and American colleagues reminded her about how strong women are and most importantly, reminded her that she wasn't alone. She shared about how connecting with Sharon, her Sseko Sister in Uganda who shares her passion for sewing and being a mother and fighting for a healthy marriage and doing work *that matters*, taught her we're not that different after all.

And in a holy moment on the sacred ground of a factory floor, through tears, she thanked our production team. She thanked them for showing up. For working hard. For risking judgement from their communities to come to work each day and do "men's work." She thanked them for bringing their best, most creative selves to work each day so she could sell products she believed in and build a business she was proud of back home. She thanked our veteran team members for their expertise and faithfulness to our mission. And she thanked our university-bound women for dreaming boldly and for inspiring and encouraging her teenage daughter back home in rural Pennsylvania to dream audaciously, in the face of criticism and disbelief, about attending MIT and someday leading a mission to Mars. She thanked them all for lighting a spark in her that gave her the courage she needed to show up in her own marriage and career and life.

And with hot tears streaming down my face, I watched a room full of Ugandan women, many whom have been told most of their lives that they have nothing to offer, or perhaps worse, that their "role" in relationship to Westerners is to be grateful beneficiaries, sit up a little taller and receive gratitude so raw and sincere and true that there was really no choice but to own their role in helping a sister find her way home again.

* * *

By all means, Pluckies!
Go!
Give!
March!
Donate!
Volunteer!

But don't forget that you were created for more than just those things. And those you're "helping"? They certainly weren't created to only receive. We're all created in the image of The Divine to partake in the beautiful and terrifying dance of giving and receiving, joy and disappointment, miracles and mistakes.

We don't need you to be anyone else's hero. We just need more people walking one another home. And when we do, we'll find that the ordinary things of French fries for breakfast and shaky words of gratitude become sacred souvenirs from the journey we were made for.

Conclusion

You Are

Well, Pluckies. Here we are at the end of this journey. But before we officially say goodbye, I want to take you back to the time when I first heard the words upon which the entire premise of this book rests.

You have everything you need to go build an extraordinary life of purpose and impact. Beginner's Pluck is less about striving and achieving and grasping and more about being courageous and intentional about getting *back* to who *you* were created to be.

You are worthy.
You are a unique and irreplaceable part of The Whole.
You are created on purpose and for a purpose.
You are.

✳ ✳ ✳

As I was entering into high school, my family situation was degrading pretty swiftly. After several years of apologies and second chances and more secrets, we were barely hanging on by a thread. My family's particular brand of brokenness was perhaps slightly more Jerry Springer than what you tend to find in the upwardly mobile, white suburbs in the Bible Belt, but like the Nice Family that we were, while our little world was crashing down around us with infidelity and financial woes and double lives, we carefully tip-toed around the broken shards of shattered hearts and (mostly) managed to look pretty as a postcard to the world around us.

This was a good technique for keeping up appearances but managed to wreak havoc on my teenage heart. The survival tactic was loud and clear: keep your mess to yourself. Fake it, even when you're not sure you're going to make it.

In addition to navigating the waters of broken trust and betrayal, I felt *deeply* ashamed. I somehow managed to run in a crowd that mostly came from beautiful, stable families. And while, as an adult, I can see what an absolute blessing it was for me to see healthy behaviors modeled in other homes, at the time it contributed to a mounting sense of shame that I was the *only* broken one. That I was the only one who had secrets to keep.

I learned to keep the mess and grief and confusion and humiliation hidden. It was safer to pretend that I was okay and that life was grand, so that's exactly what I did.

Eventually that broken trust and grief and betrayal gave way to anger. I'd lie awake at night, unsure how to express my rage in the fragile ecosphere I found myself in, so I'd dig my nails into the back of my left hand until I bled, because while it wasn't safe to direct my anger where it actually belonged, the physical manifestation of my pain felt just and satisfying.

During this season of life, I started exploring my faith, and I will never forget the day I read a particular verse of Scripture in the Gospel of Matthew.

"But if you do not forgive others their sins, your Father will not forgive your sins."*

I remember reading those words and feeling my heart sink. At that moment, offering forgiveness felt entirely outside of the realm of possibility. I simply couldn't imagine a time where my heart wouldn't be riddled with anger and resentment. And upon reading this Scripture, I was devastated to realize that this would preclude me from experiencing forgiveness myself.

For months, I was too ashamed and scared to talk to anyone about "my discovery." So, I didn't.

And then I received an invitation from a friend to come to some kind of special event her youth group was hosting. I said yes because all my girlfriends were going and when you're 16 that is literally all you need to know before you say yes to anything.

What I said yes to was a Good Friday event and a reenactment of the crucifixion of Jesus. We drove to the address listed on the invitation and parked our cars along a residential street. We then walked for what felt like a long distance down a winding drive and eventually ended up in a wooded backyard where the event took place.

I grew up in a casually Catholic family who never missed an Easter Service so Jesus on the cross was not a new story for me.

At the end of the silent reenactment set to music, they passed out index cards and pencils, and the youth leaders asked us

*Matthew 6:15 NIV.

215

to write whatever we wanted to "leave behind at the foot of Jesus's cross."

Like any cool, image-conscious teenager, I remained unaffected and above the pageantry of it all, but when given the opportunity to secretly and silently confess this burden I had been carrying, I couldn't resist.

So, I started to write. I covered both sides of the index card and then kept flipping it back and forth, writing layers upon layers until the entire card was a completely illegible mess of smeared graphite scribble.

The event came to a close and eventually my friends slowly started to get up from the blankets on the grass to leave, dropping their index cards in a white bucket sitting at the base of the giant wooden cross. With whispered hushes, they made their way back down the winding drive and toward the street where our cars were parked.

One by one, they left, and I was glad for it. I was far too fragile and knew that my reputation as the cool, spunky girl who hated sappy chick flicks and who laughed loudly but never, ever cried was on the line here.

So, while one by one they quietly got up and left, I stayed.

And I kept writing. About my anger. My shame. My broken heart. And about my fear that my anger and lack of forgiveness would keep me from the love of Jesus that I knew just barely enough of to know I desperately wanted more.

Once nearly everyone had left, I folded up that index card as many times as I could and placed it in the bucket. And despite the fact that it was entirely illegible, my hands shook as I let the card go. They shook from fear of even the slightest possibility that someone would find that card and discover me as the hateful and angry person I really was. I desperately didn't want to be discovered, but nor did I want to carry around that four-by-six-inch admission of my brokenness. So, I left it behind instead.

As the backyard grew quiet and still with only a few people milling about, I finally started my way down the long, wooded path toward the street. By this time, the private road was completely abandoned and I, thankfully, walked alone.

Until I couldn't walk any further.

Despite my best effort and practice, desperate sobs started to escape. The heaviness of it all—the secret shame and the anger and the pretending—all felt like too much to bear, and I stepped off the pavement and fell to my knees at the edge of the woods that lined the road.

With my head in my hands, I wept. I'm not sure for how long. I wept, perhaps for the first time since the cracks started to emerge many years before. I wept for myself and my family and for the broken hearts that I thought could never, ever be whole and trusting again. I wept for the Great Love I'd heard rumblings of but thought I couldn't access because of my own anger and brokenness.

I never heard anyone approach me. Surely, if I had, I would have hurriedly wiped away my tears and pretended I had dropped something. But suddenly, in the midst of my weeping, I felt an arm reach across my hunched shoulders. I was too ashamed to show myself but too broken to move away. So, with my face still buried in my hands, I leaned into whoever had their arm around me. And when I did, they supported my weight in a full embrace. I kept crying until I finally managed to catch my breath, still not knowing who this person who held me was, but I think assuming it was one of my friends with whom I had come.

With my face still buried in my hands, I said between sobs, "How can I possibly ever be forgiven when I know *I* can't ever forgive?"

As I continued to cry, there was silence. The silence confirmed what I had already suspected: I couldn't be. I was too broken. Too angry. Too far gone.

There was something sobering about this confirmation, and I stopped crying and just quietly continued to hold my hands over my face.

And then, punctuating the verdict of silence, I heard the two words in response to my question that changed me forever:

"You are."

I was startled to hear a man's voice and took my hands off my face and opened my eyes to see Jesus himself. Actual, literal Jesus, you guys. Or at least the guy who played him in the program that night. Jesus, still dressed in a costume-y, tattered white sheet and strappy leather sandals.

As I looked up and we made eye contact, he said it again:

"You are."

You are.
You are.
You are.

You are forgiven.
You are enough.
You are worthy of good things and of Great Love.

Not if.
Not when.
Not someday.

No conditions.
No exceptions.
No fine print.

Not should be.
Not would be.
Not could be.

Just . . .

"You are."

In that moment of utter brokenness, he didn't feel the need to go into an exegetical lesson on my misguided reading of Matthew 6:15 or hand me a pamphlet on how to earn Great Love. He didn't teach me how to say the right thing or urge me to clean up my mess. He didn't tell me about all my "potential" and how I really was made for more than being a sobbing, snotty pile on the side of the road.

He just held an angry, broken, scared 16-year-old with dirty knees and a splotchy, red, mascara-streaked face and said over and over again

"You are."

* * *

If you take away anything from this journey, let it be this: You are not a mass of "potential" waiting to be either wasted or realized. You don't need to earn the right or receive permission to live a life of purpose and passion and impact. To hold space for The Shadows. And to shine your light brilliantly bright.

You are.

You can stop striving, stop grasping, stop achieving, stop trying to just barely stay above water, stop running someone else's race. And instead you can get on with the joyful and gut-wrenching and life-giving and courageous work of becoming who you *already are*, underneath the costume you constructed for yourself along the way.

You are.

A Passion *Builder* and a Dreamer

A Curious Question Asker and Problem Finder

A Lover of Surprises and a Miracle Hunter

A First-Step Taker, a Good Promise Maker

with a WOW upon your lips.

A wonderfully average yet irreplaceably unique part of
    The Whole

Cracked and bruised from The Shadows

But still here

to shine brilliantly bright

and walk one another home.

Acknowledgments

You'd think the 60,000 or so words they gave me to write this book would be plenty, but there are a million more I could write about the people who have profoundly influenced this journey. This is just a tiny sliver of my gratitude.

To Mom, Dad, Pat, and Alex: thank you for shaping me and loving me. You were my first understanding of home and my launch pad. What a gift. If given the choice, I'd choose each of you over and over again. I love you. (Mom, your formal tribute lies mostly in chapter 1 but your constant love is the backdrop to the entire story.)

To the bonus family that came as a package deal with the husband: I love you three with my whole heart. I am the luckiest.

To every one of you who opened your home to a coupla sandal peddlers, hosted trunk shows, bought our products, introduced us to your friends, or bought us Chipotle when we couldn't afford it: we think and talk about you often. Your generosity and support changed us.

To those who provided critical insight, guidance, mentorship, financial support, or all of the above: we are forever grateful for you and your belief in us. Brad and Ashley, your radical, unexpected generosity in the very earliest days inspires us to this day. We want to be like you when we grow up. A special thanks to Barb and Daryl, Diane and Chris, Clyde and Sue, Pete and Kristin, Chris and Tom, Chad and Robin, Toby and Jo, Chuck and Lauren, Jay and Rachel, Marty and Sarah, Lisa Payne, Craig Keudell, Martin Segal, the PSF team, John Friess, and Julia Plowman.

To Praxis and StarveUps: thank you for creating spaces for entrepreneurs to find wisdom and fellowship in this crazy roller coaster life we were each insane enough to choose. The ride is so much better with friends who are (usually simultaneously) laughing, weeping, and hanging on for dear life alongside you.

To my team at Baker and D. C. Jacobson: Rebekah and Nicci, thank you both for your expertise and especially for your belief in this first-time author and the vision of this project. Patti and Abby, your "Yes . . . and!" has made this SO FUN. Rachel, thank you for asking. Don, you are so good at your job and so fun to work with, but make no mistake, your GIFs are the real showstopper.

To Patricia, Juliana, and Agnes: you were the first to lay eyes on this manuscript and I am so grateful for your incredibly valuable editorial feedback and cultural critique. Thank you for your honesty, wisdom, and insight.

To the teachers and leaders and administrators and mentors who believed in the CLA girls long before I ever met them: thank you for your belief that a girl can change the world and for allowing me to be a very small part of the beautiful work you are doing day in and day out.

To the Sseko Fellows: because of you, The Dream of being able to offer employment to #everygirl came true *while* I was writing this book. I could just cry every time I think about how impossible that felt ten years ago and how each of you, in your own way, came alongside me and said, "Let's go *together*." Despite the fact that I have so. many. words (#quickstory) I actually don't have enough of them to say thank you. The sisterhood we are creating together is the stuff of my wildest dreams. To the Fellows we haven't yet met, there is room at the table. Come sit with us. Here's to more global adventures and business boot camps and truth serum and Amarula and dancing in spandex while having contractions. OK. Maybe that last one was a one-time thing. We are #bettertogether.

To Sseko HQ: you are the dream team that keeps the ship moving all the time, but *especially* when I am having babies and writing books. You are curious and compassionate and quick to laugh and easy to love. You own your craft and know your **why**. I come to work each morning, grateful for your commitment, integrity, drive, and attention to the details that truly do make the magic. I will forever be completely baffled by peoples' stories of office drama and politics; you've ruined me in the best possible way. And especially to The Old Guard: Tyler, what a ride. Your heart is pure gold. Julie, thanks for saying yes before we could even figure how to pay you. Scrappy and strappy: The Sseko Way. Bri, your YES I AM HUNGRY response is the stuff of legend and you prove every Millennial-hater wrong about everything. It's an honor to learn from you and build alongside you. Baylee, you make everything more beautiful, on every level. Brent, I am so grateful you said yes to this wild ride many moons ago. (I am also very glad we didn't have to hire a translator for the team to understand your Might Coulds.) Rachael, there is no way I could have written this book without being able to trust you completely with our product and partners. Ben, I cannot imagine working alongside a more faithful, brilliant, and committed leader. From packing sandals to strategic planning, you are what co-founder dreams are made of, and you make everything better.

To our team in Uganda: you are the heartbeat of this story and the impetus for this adventure. Thank you for being women who have light and strength and vision and integrity and creativity that literally beams across entire continents and oceans and is creating a wake of hope and possibility for women across the world that we will never quite fully understand. You are the full moon that beckons a rising tide and I can't believe I get to call you co-workers, colleagues, sisters, and friends. Aggie, your partnership humbles and inspires me. Thank you for giving us your very best. To the Old School Veterans, especially Sharon, Dora, Sylvia & Joyce: webale and nkwagala nyo nyo nyo forever and to infinity. A special thanks to Mary, Mercy, and Rebecca. Your yes to this adventure and your vision for a brighter future set this story in motion.

To the circle of strong and soft and courageous and faithful forever friends who surrounded me during this season: Alex, I can't believe I share my DNA with my best friend. You are the brave one.

Anne, Molly, Fanch, Whit, and Lou: the steadiness and plain fact of your friendship can knock me of my feet if I let it. Thank you for loving Freshman Year Liz and Campus View Liz and Newlywed Liz and Broke Liz and Boss Liz and Mom Liz and Hot Mess Liz and Way-Too-Long-Winded-Marco-Polo Liz and all the Lizzes that will be born over the next five decades of our friendship. (Maybe more, but Whit, Anne, and I will go first thanks to our Splenda consumption in college.) You each hold a part of my heart.

To Blair, Kristin, Mims, and Coco: you've cooked me food and watched my babies and loaned me eggs at 6 AM that we all knew I'd never remember to replace. You've spoken tender truth and called me on my crap and shined light into some of the darkest corners of my heart and let me into yours. You've created space for my Big Feelings and Important Opinions. You've celebrated my wins and mourned my losses and I thank you in advance for putting your own bodies in harm's way if that's what it takes to keep me from reading the one-star reviews on this book. When I wake up each day, I am moved by a dream to see women the world over be loved in the way you love me.

Joy: thank you for loving the Too Much right out of me. I actually don't think I could scare you off with my intensity if I desperately tried and this means everything. Laura, you are legend and your friendship is so much more reliable and sturdy than that container you built for our trade show booth. You were the Third Musketeer and the only one who could have survived the Bohannon Bonanza. Lisa, Kristen, and Eden, thank you for being my homes away from home. Caroline, I love making magic with you, including the cover of this book. Thank you for the generosity of your creativity, friendship, and honesty. Camille + Caz 4Eva.

To Captain Ben, Jimz, Alan, and Doc: only the Duggar daughters have more brothers than I do. Thank you for loving me and my boys so well and for being an example to my sons of Really Good Men. Also, is now an okay time to admit that letting Strider into the chicken pen was not an accident? #whoops #reconciliation.

To Miriam: never in my entire life has a friend's objectively brilliant skill set and my greatest need aligned like it did during those late, rainy nights in The Brain. Something magic happened up there, and I owe you more cashews and La Croix and suitcases full of dollar bills than I will ever be able to repay. Every word of this book is truer (and more cohesive and appropriate) because of you. You're so annoying and I love you forever.

To My Boys: Theo, when I held you for the first time, something blindingly beautiful broke open in me that can never be put back together again. Your laughter and light and tenderness and absurdity have brought me more joy than I thought my heart could contain. Will Wylder, you've been my constant companion through this wild season of life. I started writing this book while you grew and tumbled inside of me and I finished it while your fat and perfect cheeks rested on my chest. You are a place of rest and peace and utter joy in the midst of chaos. My boys, this book holds my hope for the world I want to leave to you both, knowing you'll imagine and co-create an even better future than we can. Wrong will be right when Aslan's in sight.

To My Love, Benjamin. (You get two shout-outs. Personal and professional. That's what happens when you sleep with your co-worker, I suppose. Things get weird. And awesome.) From the moment you walked down William's street, elatedly waving that yellow trespassing ticket in your hand, I knew I never wanted to adventure without you again. Your brilliance and faithfulness and vision and commitment and strength and tenderness is the thread that runs through this story. Your belief—in the hope of a brighter future, in me, in our call and ability to bring Heaven to Earth—has changed me. You push me, sometimes to the very brink of myself, to become more of who I was created to be and yet love me exactly how I am. This is a mystery I have no interest in solving. All my love I do thee give.

Jesus, your Great Love changes *everything*. As our friend Anne Lamott says, "Help. Thanks. *WOW*."

Notes

Introduction

1. "Beginner's Luck," *Wikipedia*, accessed March 20, 2019, italics added, https://en.wikipedia.org/wiki/Beginner%27s_luck.

2. Annie Dillard, *The Writing Life* (New York: HarperCollins, 1989).

Chapter 1 Own Your Average

1. "Constantin Stanislavski Quotes," *BrainyQuote*, accessed February 18, 2019, https://www.brainyquote.com/quotes/constantin_stanislavski_155177.

2. Claudia M. Mueller and Carol S. Dweck, "Praise for Intelligence Can Undermine Children's Motivation and Performance," *Journal of Personality and Social Psychology* 75, no. 2 (1998): 33–52.

3. Richard Rohr, "What Is the False Self?" Center for Action and Contemplation, August 7, 2017, https://cac.org/what-is-the-false-self-2017-08-07/.

4. Rohr, "What Is the False Self?"

Chapter 2 Stop Trying to "Find Your Passion"

1. Fredrick Buechner, *Wishful Thinking: A Theological ABC* (New York: Harper & Row, 1973), 118.

2. Antonio Machado, "Campos de Castilla," as quoted in "Paths Are Made by Walking," *The Donga-A Ilbo*, July 16, 2018, http://english.donga.com/List/3/0502/26/1389278/1.

3. "Maya Angelou Quotes," *Goodreads*, accessed February 18, 2019, https://www.goodreads.com/quotes/7273813-do-the-best-you-can-until-you-know-better-then.

Chapter 3 Dream Small

1. "The Girl Effect," YouTube video, 2:22, posted by girleffect, May 24, 2008, https://www.youtube.com/watch?v=WlvmE4_KMNw.

2. Bob Goff, Instagram post, October 22, 2018, https://www.instagram.com/p/BpPaB4Qn5FT/, emphasis added.

Chapter 4 Choose Curiosity over Criticism

1. Chimamanda Ngozi Adichie, "The Danger of a Single Story," TED video, 18:43, TEDGlobal 2009, https://www.ted.com/talks/chimamanda_adichie_the_danger_of_a_single_story.

2. Professor Dolores Albarracin and Visiting Assistant Professor Ibrahim Senay, of University of Illinois along with Kenji Noguchi, Assistant Professor at Southern Mississippi University. As presented in Sciencedaily.com, "Will We Succeed? The Science of Self-Motivation," June 1, 2010, https://www.sciencedaily.com/releases/2010/05/100528092021.htm.

3. Daniel H. Pink, *To Sell Is Human* (New York: Penguin Group, 2012), 100.

4. Erica Briscoe and Jacob Feldman, "Conceptual Complexity and the Bias/Variance Tradeoff," *Cognition* 118 (2011): 2–16, https://ruccs.rutgers.edu/images/personal-jacob-feldman/papers/briscoe_feldman.pdf.

5. S. von Stumm and P. L. Ackerman, "Investment and Intellect: A Review and Meta-analysis," *Psychological Bulletin* 139, no. 4 (July 2013): 841–69, https://www.ncbi.nlm.nih.gov/pubmed/23231531.

Chapter 5 Be on Assignment in Your Own Life

1. UIS, "Leaving No One Behind: How Far on the Way to Universal Primary and Secondary Education?" UNESCO Digital Library, July 2016, unesdoc.unesco.org/ark:/48223/pf0000245238.

2. "The World's Women 2015: Trends and Statistics," United Nations Statistics Division, accessed February 14, 2019, https://unstats.un.org/unsd/gender/worlds-women.html.

3. Dr. Haidong Wang et al., "Global, Regional, and National Levels of Neonatal, Infant, and Under-5 Mortality during 1990–2013: A Systematic Analysis for the Global Burden of Disease Study," *The Lancet* 384, no. 9947 (September 13, 2014): 957–79.

4. Cheryl Doss et al, "Gender Inequalities in Ownership and Control of Land in Africa: Myths versus Reality, IFPRI Discussion Paper 01308," International Food Policy Research Institute, December 2013, http://ebrary.ifpri.org/cdm/ref/collection/p1573 8coll2/id/127957.

5. "The World's Women 2015: Trends and Statistics."

6. "Youth Employment in Africa," African Development Bank.

Chapter 6 Find and Replace

1. C. W. Churchman, "Wicked Problems," *Management Science* 14, no. 4 (1967): B-141–42.

2. "Charles Kettering Quotes," *BrainyQuote*, accessed February 18, 2019, https://www.brainyquote.com/quotes/charles_kettering_181210.

3. *Oxford Dictionary*, s.v. "confirmation bias," https://en.oxforddictionaries.com/definition/confirmation_bias.

Chapter 8 Get Your Steps In

1. Ministry of Animal Agriculture, Animal Industries and Fishing (MAAIF), "The National Livestock Census: A Summary Report of the National Livestock Census, 2008," Uganda Bureau of Statistics (UBOS), 2009, catalog.ihsn.org/index.php/catalog/3788/download/52466.

Chapter 9 Get Hooked on Making (and Keeping!) Promises

1. Robert Frost, "A Servant to Servants," *North of Boston* (New York: H. Holt and Company, 1915), italics added.

2. Supposedly Abraham Lincoln said this. The internet is giving me conflicting information on where this quote originated, but I like to think of it coming from him. Gravitas, you know?

3. G. T. Doran, "There's a S.M.A.R.T. Way to Write Management's Goals and Objectives," *Management Review* 70, no. 11 (1981): 35–36.

Chapter 10 Be Good with Good Enough

1. "Perfect Is the Enemy of Good," *Wikipedia*, accessed March 1, 2019, https://en.wikipedia.org/wiki/Perfect_is_the_enemy_of_good.

2. Seth Godin, "The Myth of Preparation," September 13, 2010, https://seths.blog/2010/09/the-myth-of-preparation/.

Chapter 11 Stop, Drop, and WOW

1. B. J. Fogg, "Fogg Method: 3 Steps to Changing Behavior," *Fogg Method*, accessed February 18, 2019, http://www.foggmethod.com/.

Chapter 12 Dream to Attract Your Team

1. "Ben Franklin Effect," *Wikipedia*, accessed February 18, 2019, https://en.wikipedia.org/wiki/Ben_Franklin_effect.

2. Jon Jecker and David Landy, "Liking a Person as a Function of Doing Him a Favour," *SAGE* 22, no. 4 (August 1969): 371–78, https://journals.sagepub.com/doi/abs/10.1177/001872676902200407.

3. Yu Nilya, "Does a Favor Request Increase Liking Toward the Requester?" *The Journal of Social Psychology* 156, no. 2 (2016): 211–21, https://www.tandfonline.com/doi/abs/10.1080/00224545.2015.1095706.

4. Brené Brown, "Shame Resilience Theory: A Grounded Theory Study on Women and Shame," *Sage Journals* 87, no. 1 (2006).

Chapter 13 Don't Hide from The Shadows

1. C. S. Lewis, *The Lion, the Witch and the Wardrobe* (New York: HarperCollins, 1950), 86.

2. C. S. Lewis, *The Four Loves* (New York: Harcourt Brace, 1991), 121.

Chapter 14 Walk One Another Home

1. Ram Dass, Facebook post, May 6, 2017, https://www.facebook.com/babaramdass/posts/1518458671519526.

About the Author

Liz Forkin Bohannon is the founder of the socially conscious fashion company Sseko Designs. In addition to being the creative director and visionary behind the brand, she leads a global team of Dreamers and Doers, including international artisan partners, staff in Portland, and the impact entrepreneurs all across the U.S. who are building the brand alongside her. Liz and the Sseko story have been featured in *Vogue*, *Marie Claire*, *InStyle*, *Fortune*, and others. In addition to running her company, Liz is a highly sought-after public speaker who travels the world speaking on the topics that light her up and inspire others to build lives of purpose and impact. Among other notable honors, Liz was named a top public speaker by Forbes, a top Transformational Leader by John Maxwell, and a social entrepreneur to watch by *Bloomberg Businessweek*. Liz lives in Portland, Oregon, where she runs Sseko, lives in an intentional community, and raises her two sons with her husband, best friend, and company co-founder, Ben.

JOIN THE SSEKO STORY

Become a Sseko Fellow and build a life (and business!) of purpose and impact.
SSEKODESIGNS.COM/SSEKO-FELLOWS

FIND YOUR COMMUNITY
Receive support and mentorship from like-minded women.

MAKE AN IMPACT
Contribute to creating opportunities for women globally.

EARN AN INCOME
Set your own schedule, enjoy Sseko product perks, and earn an income!

CARISA
Sseko Fellow, Las Vegas

"As a stay-at-home mom of three small children, I felt it was impossible for my impact to leave my four walls. But with Sseko, in addition to making incredible friends, it is truly fulfilling to know that together we are making an impact here in the U.S. and globally. And it doesn't hurt that I am earning an income and building a stunning (and sustainable!) wardrobe while I'm at it!"

COMMUNITY · IMPACT · INCOME

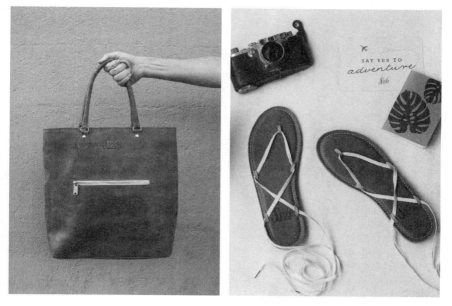

Pluckies! Stay in touch at:

WWW.LIZBOHANNON.CO

✉ liz@lizbohannon.co

◉ @lizbohannon

🐦 @lizbohannon

f facebook.com/lizforkinbohannon

Top 20 Speaker   Transformational Leader   Featured Speaker

——————— AS SEEN IN ———————

LIKE THIS
BOOK?
Consider sharing it with others!

- Share or mention the book on your social media platforms. Use the hashtag **#BeginnersPluck**.

- Write a book review on your blog or on a retailer site.

- Pick up a copy for friends, family, or anyone who you think would enjoy and be challenged by its message!

- Share this message on Twitter, Facebook, or Instagram: **I loved #BeginnersPluck by @LizBohannon // @ReadBakerBooks**

- Recommend this book for your church, workplace, book club, or class.

- Follow Baker Books on social media and tell us what you like.

 ReadBakerBooks

 ReadBakerBooks

 ReadBakerBooks